Enjoy the read!

What People are Saying about *The Subscription Playbook*

"A must-read for anyone thinking of subscription pricing in their business. I wish we had this book at Catch!"

— Gabby Leibovich, Co-Founder of Catch, Scoopon, Eatnow/Menulog

"If you are ready to finally understand how not just to scale a company but also how to attract investment, then this book is for you. Subscription works and the idea of creating a 'moat' around your business to keep customers engaged and happy is simply brilliant. This book will challenge you to rethink your business model and to build a sustainable business that can go from 'good' to 'outstanding.' It will show you how to create predictable cash flow and teach you the specific steps to make it happen. A must-read and one of the best business books I have read."

— Andrew Roberts, Award-Winning Business Coach and Advisor to Fast-Growth Companies

"Deeper client relationships and more predictable finances lie at the heart of every entrepreneur's dreams, and subscription business models are the answer. Robert Coorey unpacks in detail the strategies and tactics needed to build a successful and sustainable subscription business."

— Peter Sheahan, Best-Selling Author and C-Suite Advisor

"Robert lives his talk and is the real deal when it comes to sharing the best in the market. This book is exactly that. The best secrets and tips to build subscriptions that last. Highly recommended."

— Sam Cawthorn, Former Australian of the Year and International Best-Selling Author

"Robert Coorey makes an inarguable case for why subscription is the answer to your business' financial wellbeing while providing your clients with what they need again and again. Backed up with countless case studies and Coorey's personal experiences, *The Subscription Playbook* is the playbook for the game you want to play and win."

> — **Tyler R. Tichelaar, PhD and Award-Winning Author of** *The Nomad Editor: Living the Lifestyle You Want, Doing Work You Love*

"If you're looking to solidify income streams, reinforce your credibility, and lead with value through a subscription model, but you're not sure where to start or quite what to do, Robert Coorey's *The Subscription Playbook* contains everything you need to know. Written in lively, engaging prose, chock-full of practical, real-world examples, and overflowing with actionable advice, this book has to be on the 'must read' list of every aspiring entrepreneur. Heartily recommended."

> — **Gary Bloomer, Marketing Advisor**

This book had me hooked from the first line. While I've read lots of marketing books and taken numerous courses, Robert Coorey always has a different perspective. He surprises with clever ideas and new hacks that you can use to grow your business quickly and sustainably. Robert Coorey thinks like no one else. *The Subscription Playbook* is packed with real stories and so many insights that I felt compelled to scribble notes on every page. '

> — **Rebekah Campbell, Entrepreneur and Author**

THE SUBSCRIPTION PLAYBOOK

How to Build a Rock-Solid Recurring Revenue Stream

Robert Coorey, MBA

THE SUBSCRIPTION PLAYBOOK

How to Build a Rock-Solid Recurring Revenue Stream

Copyright © 2022 by Robert Coorey. All rights reserved.

Published by:

Aviva Publishing

Lake Placid, NY

(518) 523-1320

www.AvivaPubs.com

All Rights Reserved. No part of this book may be used or reproduced in any manner whatsoever without the expressed written permission of the author. Address all inquiries to https://www.thesubscriptionplaybook.com

Limit of Liability/Disclaimers of Warranty: While the publisher and author have used their best efforts in preparing this book, they make no representations or warranties with respect to the accuracy or completeness of the contents of this book and specifically disclaim any implied warranties of merchantability or fitness for a particular purpose. No warranty may be created or extended by sales representatives or written sales materials. The advice and strategies contained herein may not be suitable for your situation. You should consult with a professional where appropriate. Neither the publisher nor author shall be liable for any loss of profit or any other commercial damages, including but not limited to special, incidental, consequential, or any other damages.

ISBN: 978-1-63618-240-7

Library of Congress Control Number: 2022915744

Editor: Tyler Tichelaar, Superior Book Productions

Cover Design: Paloma

Interior Book Layout: PixelStudio

Every attempt has been made to properly source all quotes.

First Edition

2 4 6 8 10 12

DEDICATION

This book is dedicated to my wife Dianna, with love.

Thank you for giving me encouragement and always supporting me.

5 Reasons to Read This Book
(even if you don't have a subscription business)

1. Almost any business can add subscription billing. Traditional small businesses such as doctors, lawyers, and restaurants are starting to use subscription billing. Even hairdressers are turning to subscription billing, offering a bundle of services for a flat monthly fee.
2. Subscription billing businesses are easier to sell than one-time revenue businesses. One day every small business owner gets tired of their business and wants to sell. Sadly, most can't find a buyer and simply have to close their doors. By implementing subscription billing, the business owner will have a much stronger business that is easier to sell for a higher price.
3. Customers often prefer "smoother" subscription billing to unpredictable one-off fees. My friend who runs a financial services law firm told me his clients would rather pay $3,000 a month ongoing for access to his advice than $30,000 upfront. The $3,000 a month ends up being a lot more money over the long term for the legal firm and his clients are happier.
4. There are eight different subscription models and five ways to price your subscription offering. It can be overwhelming to decide where to start. This book gives a framework on how to choose the best subscription model

and pricing for your personal situation. There are also free tools listed on the book resources page to help you.
5. Once you get some success with your subscription business, you will attract copycats and competitors. You will learn how to "dig your moat" and fortify your business from attack.

Turn the page and keep reading if you want a subscription business that works for you!

Free Book Resources Web Page

Some of the content couldn't fit on these pages, so I have collated it all into a free book resources page.

Visit https://www.subscriptionplaybook.com/resources for free access to:

1. The subscription model selector tool: Answer a few easy questions and receive a personalized recommendation about which subscription model is best suited to your business.
2. "Moat" Scorecard: A diagnostic tool where you can see how your business ranks in terms of the key factors to keep away competitors.
3. Pricing model recommendation tool: Find out which pricing model is the best fit for your business.
4. Screenshots of best practice subscription businesses.

To get all of this content and much more, go to https://www.subscriptionplaybook.com/resources

CONTENTS

Chapter One: Subscription Recurring Revenue: The Ultimate Business .. 1
    The First Major Subscription Model Success from 1926 9
    So...Why Subscription Again? 16
    Why the Subscription Model Could Benefit Your Small Business 17
    A Real Estate Example With Subscription 23
    It's Time to Build Your Subscription and Moat Model 24

Chapter Two: Choosing Your Subscription Model 27
    Model #1 – The Member Benefits Model 31
    Model #2 – The Consumables Model 33
    Model #3 – The Unlimited Content Model 35
    Model #4 – Subscription Boxes 38
    Model #5 – Bundled Services 40
    Model #6 – The Insurance Model 41
    Model #7 – Software as a Service 43
    Model #8 – Minimum Commitment 46
    Which Model Works for You? 48

Chapter Three: Choosing Your Pricing Model 49
    The Five Pricing Models to Consider 56
    Model #1 – Regular Fixed Fee Subscription 56
    Model #2 – Advertising 59
    Model #3 – E-Commerce 63
    Model #4 – Transaction Processing 66
    Model #5 – Data and APIs 68
    You Don't Have to Stick to One Model 70
    Should You Go Freemium? – The Factors to Consider 71
    Freemium vs Free Trials 73
    Annual vs Monthly Subscriptions 76
    How to Choose Your Pricing Model 79

Chapter Four: Usage-Based Pricing: The Emerging Pricing Model 81
    The Unusual Pricing Strategy Procore Uses to Scale Revenue 82
    The Miracle of Net Dollar Retention 83
    Why Are Businesses Flocking to Usage-Based Pricing? 84
    Three Key Benefits of Usage-Based Pricing 85
    Potential Downsides of Usage-Based Pricing...And How to Overcome Them 88

Two Clever Ways to Mix Usage-Based Pricing With Subscription 90
The Four Factors to Getting Usage-Based Pricing Right 91
The Evolution of the Subscription Model. 94

Chapter Five: Dig Your Moat: How to Protect Your Subscription Business From Copycats **97**

How a Startup Bank Completely Disrupted the Brazilian Banking Sector 97
MOATS—The Five Key Factors for Protecting Your Subscription Castle 102
How GoPro Added Lucrative Subscription Revenue to Its Camera Sales 102
M – Marketing Supremacy 104
O - One. 108
A – Audience 112
T – Toughness. 119
Tell-Tale Signs of a Company With a Moat 130
How Stripe Started From Scratch and Built a Powerful Moat 131
Does Your Business Fit the MOATS Framework? 135

Chapter Six: Network Effects: The Little-Known Strategy Turning Small Companies into Fortresses **137**

How Pete and Sami Transformed the Real Estate Industry and Exited for $3.5B. . . 137
Network Effects Are All Around Us 140
The Six Major Types of Network Effects 142
The Chicken or the Egg? Getting Started With Network Effects 156
One Clever Strategy a Hairdresser Marketplace Used to Grow Rapidly 158
Preventing People from Circumventing the Network 159
Gamification—Borrowing Computer Game Concepts to Increase Engagement . . 162
Gamifying Your Product—Some Quick Tips 164
Leverage the Power of Network Effects 166

Chapter Seven: Land and Expand: Lifting Revenue Without Hiring a Huge Sales Team **167**

How Patreon Stumbled Upon the Perfect Growth Engine. 168
How a Local Bakery "Lands and Expands" Into Cafés and Restaurants 171
Explaining the Land and Expand Strategy 171
The Five Factors Needed to Successfully Execute Land and Expand. 174
How Do You Know If Land and Expand Is Working? 179
Making Land and Expand Work—DocuSign's Keys to Success. 182
Prepare for Landing. 188

Chapter Eight: Quick Ways to Grow Client Numbers on a Shoestring Budget 191

The Four Techniques You Can Use to Grow Membership Numbers 192

 Technique #1 – Leverage Community Marketing............................193
 Technique #2 – Use Webinars to Attract New Members (and Retain Existing Ones) ..195
 Technique #3 – Create a Customer Referral Program 197
 Technique #4 – Use Embedded Integration to Make Your Service Indispensable 206
 How Will You Grow Your Subscription Service?............................208

Chapter Nine: How to Keep 'Em Coming Back: Minimizing Churn and Maximizing Usage... 211
 Why Net Negative Churn and Expansion Revenue Is So Appealing 213
 Reducing Churn—The Four Key Tips for Subscription Businesses 213
 How Groove Reduced Churn by 71 Percent With a Simple Email..............219
 Implementing a Modern Loyalty Program...................................221
 A Deep Dive Into Uber's Brilliant Modern Spin on Loyalty Programs 221
 Keeping Customers Happy—Best Practices for Subscription Businesses........228
 How Will You Keep and Grow Your Customer Base? 236

Chapter Ten: Are You on Track? How to Know If You Have Product/Market Fit.. 239
 Netflix's Evolution into a Subscription Model...............................240
 Looker and the Big Market Shift 241
 Patreon and the Overwhelming Customer Response........................243
 GitHub's Users Ask to Pay 244
 Superhuman—How Rahul Found Product/Market Fit for the Fastest Email in the World...245
 Making Subscription Businesses Work on Small Budgets 250
 How The Food Boss Academy Started Subscription on a Shoestring Budget.....252
 A Low-Cost Online Retailer Bolts on Subscription...........................254
 How Patrick Turned a Nine-Month "Experiment" Into a $200M Exit...........256
 How Michael Turned an Excess Stock Problem Into a Billion-Dollar Business ...259
 Some Final Advice for the Bootstrappers On Razor-Thin Budgets 262

A Final Note 265

Resources 267

Free Book Resources Web Page....................................... 287

About the Author 289

Be Sure to Read Feed a Starving Crowd 291

CHAPTER ONE

SUBSCRIPTION RECURRING REVENUE: THE ULTIMATE BUSINESS

"That's it! I'm taking our savings and putting it in a separate account you can't touch. Enough is enough!"

My wife was done.

We'd already invested more than $200,000 into my business, a "results-guaranteed" marketing agency. And we were still burning through cash faster than an American consumer on Black Friday.

I was in the weeds—all I could see was what my business could become. But my wife just saw red ink on our bank statement and our life savings evaporating.

In hindsight, she was right!

But before I tell you how this story ends, let me back up a bit to explain how I got here.

I was twenty-eight years old. I had always overachieved in the three corporate jobs I'd had up until then—selling photocopiers, banking, and telecommunications. I smashed every target thrown at me. But for some reason, I wasn't satisfied despite earning a comfortable six-figure salary, being a national sales manager, and getting my MBA. I think they call it the Entrepreneur's Curse.

You know what it's like: You're an entrepreneur at heart, working for someone else.

No matter how well you're doing, no matter how much money you earn, no matter what your job title is, you can't get that voice out of your head that says, *"You should be running your own show."*

Toward the end of one of my corporate roles, I was so tired of the organization that I physically found it hard to get out of bed in the morning to get started.

Marketing had always been a passion of mine in the corporate world. I was convinced I could help many businesses if I turned my full attention to marketing. So, I studied the best marketers closely and started running some campaigns for my dad's company. (At least I knew I would still get a Christmas present if it didn't work out.)

It turned out I was pretty good at this marketing thing!

After about a year, I wanted to work with people again. I spoke with a fast-growing digital marketing agency. It allowed me to start my own division with a few team members who were wrapping up another project. That worked out great for two years, but I *still* wasn't satisfied! I wanted to take on the world. *Damn Entrepreneur's Curse*!

I then wrote my first book, *Feed a Starving Crowd*, and started my own digital marketing agency.

So here I was, a young entrepreneur with my own business—ready to take on the world. Thanks to offering payment upon results, the company snowballed and started to attract international clients because of this innovative new business model.

I was involved in a ton of fantastic product launches. Things seemed to be going well. But while this seems like a success story at first glance—a tale of a kid using his ingenuity to succeed—this experience taught me a lesson about what was *wrong* with my approach.

In every case, the revenue I generated was a one-time thing. This worked well enough when I was brand new to the marketing world, but my marketing team grew over time, and I had overhead to cover.

The way I did business at that point meant we were always in a feast or famine cycle. We would win a few projects and max out our capacity. Then the projects would wrap up, and I'd sit there wondering how I would pay all these people.

That's a dangerous spot for any business, and many companies today are right there.

I quickly learned that relying exclusively on one-time revenue streams created much risk. As I dug into the numbers, I realized how vulnerable we were. We had no real unique point of difference from our competitors. Our margins were ridiculously low. So even though we were growing fast, we were in a precarious situation.

Until then, I could tolerate our revenue's up and down nature because I always had the safety net of our savings to draw on, but everything changed after my wife's "enough is enough" moment. I had no choice but to sell the business.

After much hustle, it turns out that one of my best clients liked the work we did for them. They kindly offered to buy some of the marketing content I had created and take on my remaining team. This allowed me to exit gracefully and hold my head high. It wasn't a great financial result for me, but at least my dignity was preserved—so I treated it as a lesson learned.

Looking back, my wife was right. If she hadn't cut me off from our savings account, my marketing business would have eventually cost us our home, and who knows what else.

It turns out I'm not the only one in this boat.

The US Bureau of Labor Statistics says about half of all businesses slam their doors shut for good within the first five years. The top reason? Low sales and bad cash flow.

My marketing business had great sales, but I could certainly relate to the "bad cash flow" part!

The stress of operating a one-time revenue business, where you live hand to mouth and ultimately close it down after years of effort, is demoralizing. And sadly, one in two business owners who begin starry-eyed and full of wonder end up at zero—or worse than zero in many cases.

This realization led to me exploring how to build the type of business I will discuss in this book:

The subscription business.

Subscriptions are all around us.

If you pay for Netflix, Amazon Prime, or Dropbox, you're using a subscription service. These types of businesses are unique. They carve out an indelible place in the market and, most importantly, *have recurring revenue from multiple sources.*

That type of business could help me sleep comfortably at night, knowing I could cover payroll the next month. And my wife would be supportive! Subscription businesses sounded like heaven to me. I needed something more sustainable, more reliable. And ever since that realization, I've studied how subscription companies establish competitive advantages and make themselves more valuable.

Then, I took what I learned and implemented these strategies in my own business.

After the "results-based agency" debacle, I joined forces with my brother. He knew how to create great software products—and I could sell and market them. The dream team!

The first product was Archistar Academy, an e-learning academy with exclusive courses for architecture and engineering students. It was a unique product with a great target audience and, best of all, recurring subscription revenue!

The academy performed so well that we decided to create software for architects and property developers. We called it Archistar Property.

When we launched Archistar Property, things took off.

We raised more than $30 million in venture capital funding in just a few short years. We were listed as the twentieth fastest-growing company in Australia by the *Australian Financial Review* (the Australian equivalent of the *Wall Street Journal*) in December 2021.

So, what led to this success?

It comes down to two factors:

- Recurring subscription revenue
- A strong moat

The combination of a subscription revenue stream and a moat is the ultimate business. In the following pages, I will explain why and give you actionable strategies you can use to create this type of business for yourself.

In the future, many organizations selling direct to consumers will offer subscription services—if you want to compete for the long run, you will need to add subscription.

But before we dig into that, we need to answer a question:

What is a moat?

If you've seen pictures of ancient castles, you've probably noticed they almost always have a deep, wide body of water surrounding them—a moat. The purpose of a moat was to protect the castle from attack.

Adding subscription revenue is a great start, but it's not enough. Just because *you* start selling dog biscuits on a subscription basis instead of ad-hoc doesn't mean I can't do the same thing. I could find a dog biscuit supplier, set up a template website overnight, and we're in competition.

Businesses need to add moat elements and subscription revenue to be safe.

In 1995, Warren Buffett was asked at the annual Berkshire Hathaway investor meeting what he looked for in businesses he invested in. He said, *"We're trying to find a business with a wide and long-lasting moat around it."*

Since then, business owners have been searching for the holy grail of building a "moat" around their business. Why are companies like Apple, Google, Microsoft, Amazon, and Netflix consistently growing and able to withstand fierce competitive attacks?

Well, they have a big focus on subscription billing and have added multiple moat elements. That makes them hard to compete with. Compare this to a standard commodity business like selling office supplies and you can quickly see which model is more appealing.

The Subscription Playbook will show you how to add subscription revenue to any business and protect it from competitive threats. This book is a combination of my personal stories and best practices from both large and small companies. I will show how even the most traditional businesses—medical practices, coffee shops, car manufacturers—can add subscription revenue.

The Subscription Model That Changed Everything

A recurring subscription business model.... It seems so obvious today, especially for software-based companies. But only in the last decade or so have we seen this model explode in popularity. At least in the software world, subscription wasn't a concept in the late '90s through 2000s. I know that from my experience working in IT support during that period.

Back then, software companies expected customers to pay an upfront fee for the software, followed by a setup fee and maybe an additional fee for support and upgrades.

Operating systems are a good example. Every few years, Microsoft would release a new version of Windows, which customers would pay a few hundred dollars for. That model worked well enough for a time. But the advent of CD burners made these complex software packages easy to pirate. The model encouraged one-time payments with no recurring revenue. You can start to see why it wasn't sustainable.

And yet, software companies followed this model for years. The one-time payment model is one businesses in many other verticals still follow, even though the subscription model has proven itself more effective.

Of course, I'm not telling you anything new here. The subscription model has existed for centuries, making it even more baffling why so many industries have been slow to adopt it.

THE FIRST MAJOR SUBSCRIPTION MODEL SUCCESS FROM 1926

Let me take you on a journey. Let's rewind almost one hundred years.

It's 1926. An entrepreneur named Harry Scherman is working on a concept for a business that would become the foundation of the subscription model we have today.

He would call this business The Book of the Month Club (BOMC).

Scherman had experimented with several models before settling on subscriptions, bringing him his most significant success. Some of the previous models proved profitable.

For example, BOMC was founded as Little Leather Library in 1916. Scherman, alongside his business partners, chose to copy a tobacco company's idea. They would provide customers with a volume of Shakespeare with every purchase of their product.

Scherman reversed the template, however. He chose to print a range of public domain titles that Little Leather Library sold, along with a small selection of chocolates. The model proved popular, with the unexpected gifts Little Leather Library offered being so desirable that the company sold 25 million copies of its books between 1916 and 1920.

But BOMC would do things differently.

Scherman devised a model where customers would subscribe to the club and receive at least four books annually, each pre-chosen from a catalog of classic and contemporary texts. Scherman understood that offering high-quality titles was key to keeping his customers engaged (and subscribed), so he hired a team of respected critics and journalists to handpick books BOMC would provide.

Scherman offered his subscriptions by direct mail.

Within the first year, BOMC had 4,000 subscribers. By the end of its second, that number had grown to 60,000. And more than twenty years later, in the aftermath of World War II, BOMC boasted an astonishing 550,000 subscribers. Each of these was a customer paying a regular fee, creating a robust recurring-revenue stream. And referring to our earlier discussion about moats, this subscription model was unlike anything that any regular bookshop of the time could offer. For a while, the subscription model was the moat BOMC used to protect its business.

The Evolution and Sale of BOMC

As time went on, BOMC began to evolve its services. For example, its Music Appreciation Records arm did the same thing BOMC did for books—only for classical records. This arm also acted as the precursor to the Columbia Record Club, which we'll get to in a moment.

By the middle of the 1950s, BOMC had more than 800,000 members, meaning the company officially had more members than the number of book titles available in all the US' many libraries combined. Scherman and his ingenious model had introduced thousands of people to books they may never have read otherwise. Following Scherman's death in 1969, the BOMC was sold for the princely sum of $63 million in 1977.

Interestingly, the BOMC is still running today. The company isn't too transparent with its current membership numbers, though it does have a popular Instagram page with more than one million followers.

Subscription Reaches Other Industries

BOMC appeared to light a subscription spark in other industries—take magazines as a perfect example. Today, we often associate the subscription model with magazines. But for over a century after the birth of the magazine industry, subscriptions weren't considered. Most magazines made their money from charging more per copy than it cost to produce the magazine.

In this case, the rise of advertising changed everything.

Once magazine publishers started making millions of dollars from the ads they placed on their pages, subscriptions became a viable model. The publishers could set subscription prices below the cost of production because they knew they'd get the money back (and then some) through ads. It may sound a little cynical, but magazine subscriptions essentially became subscriptions to receive the magazine's content and view the advertisements inside! Magazines were selling attention.

Of course, we see subscription models in so many other businesses.

Take gyms, for example.

Most gyms charge monthly membership fees—often as high as $100 or more per month. These subscriptions are sold on the dream of attaining a slimmer waistline or building bigger muscles. Gyms sell access to required equipment and can generate recurring revenue from the fact that they own it.

But the gym subscription model also has some interesting quirks.

Most gyms can't support the number of members they have. About 80 percent of people who sign up for a gym membership cancel within six months, and 50 percent never make it through the gym's doors. They just subscribe and never go—which may sound familiar to anyone nursing a neglected gym membership card in their wallet right now. On average, to stay profitable, gyms need up to ten times more paying members than they can support at any one time.

It's possible.

Plenty of gyms do it.

But it's not the safest of subscription models out there.

And this brings us to an important point.

The subscription model is a powerful one—but it's also possible to fail with this model if you take an unsustainable approach. This possibility of failure is the reason we incorporate the moat aspect into our ultimate model. Without a moat, a subscription business can be just as vulnerable as any other.

Adding subscription revenue is a great start but not enough. Remember my dog biscuit example? Businesses need to add moat elements and subscription revenue to be safe.

Just ask the Columbia Record Club....

From $1.4 Billion in Annual Profit to Complete Collapse

Columbia Record Club's big business idea was simple.

It looked at what BOTM was doing and decided to replicate it for music. Columbia created a catalog of albums, sent it out to potential customers, and offered them an opportunity to choose one for free.

People love "free," so the offer was snapped up by so many that the company boasted a membership of 128,000 people within a year. And in 1963, just two years later, Columbia shipped more than 7 million records annually. To give you a sense of the true scale of its success, those 7 million records accounted for 10 percent of all records sold in the United States at the time. By the 1990s, when Columbia hit its peak annual earnings of $1.4 billion, similar subscription services accounted for 15 percent of all US record sales.

It's easy to see why Columbia succeeded.

The company maintained a colossal catalog of artists and records, offering enough variety for fans of any music genre. It also made buying music convenient. Instead of dragging yourself to a music store, you could just select a bunch of titles from a catalog from the comfort of your home. There wasn't even any fussing with cash or credit cards because your subscription took care of everything for you.

Columbia even bolstered its chances of success by analyzing the data it collected about its customers and their music choices. In doing so, Columbia became one of the first companies in the world to start using data processing to anticipate trends in the music industry.

If this all sounds familiar, it's because these are the reasons today's extensive subscription services succeed. The likes of Netflix and Spotify offer enormous variety, use data to direct users toward titles or songs they're likely to enjoy, and offer a level of convenience unparalleled by anything that came before them.

With all of this going for it, we have an obvious question.

Why did Columbia Record House fail?

In a word: greed.

Okay, that may be oversimplifying it a little, but one of the biggest reasons Columbia failed is it leaned too much into its focus on acquiring customers. The strategy that had worked so well for decades began to backfire—too much emphasis on getting new customers, not enough on providing a quality service to existing customers.

Do you remember those free records Columbia used so effectively in the early days?

People would jump at the chance to get records for free (or nearly free). But they wouldn't realize they were tying themselves to a subscription they didn't want. So, they'd receive the next batch of records at full price. Columbia actively made its subscription process less transparent than it should have been.

It did a great job of angering a lot of potential customers.

Then, combine that with the fact that Columbia failed to protect its moat. For decades, physical media dominated the music industry, which was critical to the success of the Columbia model. The advent of MP3s, peer-to-peer file sharing, and eventually, streaming broke its model.

SO...WHY SUBSCRIPTION AGAIN?

I'm sharing this Columbia story because you need to see that the subscription model isn't infallible. Bad practices and an inability to adapt to a market's changing needs can (and will) result in a shrinking moat to the point where it isn't even there anymore.

But when done well...

And when combined with a strong moat...

The subscription model changes *everything*!

Recurring subscription revenue isn't just for software. Thanks to Software-as-a-Service (SaaS) and streaming, subscriptions have become the gold standard. Subscriptions can work for nearly any business if you have a product or a service that people buy often and enjoy.

I'll give you an example.

I have a favorite type of peppermint tea.

Each month, I automatically receive a shipment of that tea from Amazon, saving 10 percent on what I would have paid if I had made a one-time buy. Tea is a product I want. It's a product I need to buy over and over to maintain stock. So, it's perfect for the subscription model.

A lot of other companies are discovering the benefit of recurring revenue for their consumer products. You can now buy supplements, subscription boxes, and razor blades via subscription. We have companies like Loot Crate and the Dollar Shave Club showing us that subscriptions can work for various products.

Maybe it can work for you, too.

WHY THE SUBSCRIPTION MODEL COULD BENEFIT YOUR SMALL BUSINESS

Let's switch focus to salability.

Most owners of small- and medium-sized businesses have a vague plan when they start their companies. The goal is generally to build something that can support their lifestyle—and eventually, when it's time to retire, sell the company and live off the profits.

It's the business owner's dream.

But it's also a dream that doesn't always come to fruition as many small and medium business owners would like it to. Those who base their business models around one-time transactions will find it increasingly hard to sell their companies for what they believe they're worth.

Imagine spending decades of your life building a business, pouring your heart and soul into making it successful, only to end up unable to reap the rewards.

It's heartbreaking.

And the reason is a concept we touched on earlier:

Predictability.

That is where most businesses based on one-time transactions struggle. You'll likely find most potential acquirers will only offer two to seven times your net profit for this type of business (assuming you get an offer at all). You're much more likely to see offers at the low end of the scale if you rely on one-time transactions.

Subscription businesses, on the other hand...

We only need to look at the sale of Slack to Salesforce to see the difference. Salesforce paid about twenty-six times Slack's projected revenue (yes, *projected revenue*, not even actual current revenue, and certainly not net profit) to get its hands on the company.

My point is net profit doesn't even come into the equation for many subscription businesses. And to highlight just how different the numbers look when you compare subscription businesses to the average small business, I have a few statistics to share.

Spot the Difference

Average small business owner	Slack
$387k in revenue	$867m in revenue
Business is sold for $320,000 on average	Sold for $28b to Salesforce
< 2% chance of ever selling the business.	Acquired
Sale price to revenue multiple 0.67x	Sale price to *projected* revenue multiple 26x

Sadly, 98 percent of small businesses close their doors instead of getting acquired. Small business owners are like troops deployed to No Man's Land in World War I. They're brave and valiant, but the odds are stacked against their survival.

The typical small business is theoretically worth $320,000 on average. You could make the same company anywhere from five to thirty times as valuable by moving to subscription because subscription businesses are usually valued on revenue instead of profit. A subscription business with a strong moat can be worth hundreds of millions, or billions, of dollars.

That's a big difference.

Businesses that have powerful moats sell for millions, if not *billions*. Companies that don't have a moat sell for far less. That's the difference between having a moat and not having one. And this book is intended to act as your playbook for building a subscription business with a powerful moat.

The Other Reason Small Businesses Aren't as Valuable

Building on everything above, there's another reason small businesses aren't appealing to potential buyers:

They're often dependent on the founder or CEO.

We've all heard people talk about how you should work "on" the business, not "in" it. The prospect of working "in" the business is one most buyers don't like. They don't want to buy a full-time job—they want to invest in a robust company that allows them to focus on strategy and direction.

Investors don't want a business they can work "on." They want one they can work "over."

What do "in," "on," and "over" mean in the context of business?

Imagine you're running a coffee shop.

If you're working "in" the business, you collect the money, make the coffee, sweep the floors, and order supplies. You do all the day-to-day stuff required to keep the business working.

If you work "on" the business, you elevate yourself above the day-to-day. Instead, you focus on more strategic tasks, such as hiring team members and creating processes.

But the person who works "over" the business…

That person sees and works to achieve the big picture. They may create a chain of coffee stores. They'll be focused on opening locations in strategic areas and acquiring other stores to scale. When you work "over" the business, you're free from the minutia of the day-to-day. You're focusing on what you can do to grow.

From working with hundreds of business owners over the years, I can safely say most business owners are working "in" the business. A small percentage are working "on" the business. And very few are working "over" the business.

I'll be the first to admit I've been guilty of this.

Early in my career, I thought I was clever by doing my own admin and handling the day-to-day operations. I was "saving money." Looking back, this was some of the most expensive time I have ever spent. It's an opportunity cost you can't get back. As time goes on, with more experience, I've learned to get better at empowering my team.

But it's been a journey.

And completing that journey requires you to change your mindset on what a business owner is....

For some reason, I always thought I could do everything better myself. I could have just done it by the time I trained someone how to do something.

Then one day, roughly ten years ago, I had an epiphany on the way to the office.

I thought about every company in the country. They were doing all the operational functions just fine with their teams. Each company could create a product or service, advertise it, sell it, collect the money, and service the customers.

And here I was, thinking I was the only person who could do everything.

Crazy!

When I did business coaching, one of the first exercises I had my clients do was to log every activity they did in a week. And when we'd review their activity, they would usually get angry with themselves about how they were spending their time. Despite the frustration, it was always a great exercise because, without awareness, it's hard to make any changes.

So...

Let's do that exercise!

ACTION EXERCISE:

Maintain a log of all your business activities over the next week.

With the log completed, work out what percentage of your time is spent working "in," "on," and "over" the business.

You're probably going to see a lot more time spent "in" than time spent "on" or "over."

With that log in hand, dedicate the next week to making some improvements. Try to spend a little more time in the "over" section.

Here's a hint...

Implementing the strategies I share in this book will help you spend a lot more time in the "over" category, allowing you to build your subscription business with a moat.

Top 10 Activities	Time Spent
_____	_____
_____	_____
_____	_____
_____	_____
_____	_____
_____	_____
_____	_____
_____	_____
_____	_____
_____	_____

A REAL ESTATE EXAMPLE WITH SUBSCRIPTION

Let me give you an example.

You have a real estate agency you're trying to sell. A buyer shows some interest and wants to look at the books.

What are they going to look at first?

Your rent book—the rent from your rental properties.

Why?

Because they want to see the business can generate recurring revenue. The property sale transactions are tremendous and can add to the company's value, but they're all one-time transactions. There's no guarantee the business will achieve the same number of sales transactions in any given year, making sales revenue unstable.

Revenue in the rent book is stable and recurring, meaning it's a much better indicator of the strength of your business.

A lot of real estate companies are picking up on this. Take, for example, :Different, a fast-growing Australian real estate technology company. The marketing message on its website is:

"Proactive property management for just $30/week."

It's shooting for the recurring revenue that property management brings because it knows that's where the stable money is. And investors agree! :Different has raised tens of millions of dollars from investors and has a promising future.

So, we need to look at subscriptions to make your business more stable as a revenue-driving asset and to make your business more attractive to potential investors or buyers.

IT'S TIME TO BUILD YOUR SUBSCRIPTION AND MOAT MODEL

The subscription business model isn't the only effective one out there. There are terrific businesses listed on the New York

Stock Exchange that leverage usage-based and transactional pricing models.

We will dig into those models later in the book and compare them.

But I'll tell you this...

If I'm starting a new business tomorrow, recurring subscription revenue with a moat is the model I will work toward. It's what business buyers and investors look for...and it helps you sleep soundly at night!

You just need to know how to make the model work.

And that's where this book comes in.

Get ready for the ride!

CHAPTER TWO

CHOOSING YOUR SUBSCRIPTION MODEL

So, we know subscriptions are a brilliant business model.

You get a sustainable and recurring income stream through subscriptions. Not only does that make for a more robust business during your ownership, but it also means your business will be more attractive to buyers when you decide it's time to leave.

I'll dig into the specifics of building a moat around your subscription business in a moment.

But before that, we have a big question to answer...

What sort of subscription business should you build?

Subscription isn't always as simple as knocking up some membership tiers, slapping prices on them, and calling it a day. There are a bunch of twists and variations (eight in total) you need to think about.

Choose the right subscription model and you're on your way to building a fantastic business.

Choose the wrong one…

Well, let's not think about that!

I want to tell you about a company with a fantastic subscription model: GoPro.

"What's that?" you might ask.

"GoPro? Those are the guys who make the cameras, right? Their stuff is good, but surely their business is the exact type you just told us to steer clear of. They sell one-off products!"

You're right…

Kind of!

Although GoPro made its name by manufacturing small, durable cameras that shoot high-quality footage in precarious conditions, it doesn't make all of its money from those cameras.

A good chunk of its revenue comes from something else: its subscription service.

In 2016, GoPro rolled out its first version. For just $4.99 per month, subscribers got unlimited cloud storage.

Not a bad deal.

After all, the photo and video quality of cameras are so high that storage and backup are an ongoing challenge. Thanks to the people who built your camera, access to cloud storage has to be an attractive option.

And it is!

Take the growth the company experienced in 2020 as an example.

GoPro had a goal of reaching between 600,000 and 700,000 subscribers by the end of 2020—and they smashed it. By the end of the year, they had 750,000 people enrolled.

As I write this, GoPro's subscription service keeps growing. It's at 1.74 million users at the end of May 2022, meaning the company has more than doubled its new subscribers.

And the new subscription offers a lot more than the first version did.

Now, users get cloud storage. But they also get dedicated editing tools, deals on new GoPro equipment, and, in some cases, replacements for their existing equipment. The company has also streamlined its service, meaning a GoPro subscription only costs $49.99 per year (as of 2022).

Let's do some math.

1.16 million subscribers multiplied by $49.99 is…

$86,982,600 *per year.*

GoPro created an eight-figure recurring revenue stream in about five years using a subscription model.

They were the first photography hardware company to go this route. And after seeing those numbers, you can bet they won't be the last.

So, why am I telling you this story?

Simple.

Most people would look at GoPro and see a hardware manufacturer that couldn't possibly take advantage of a subscription model. The brilliant minds at GoPro thought differently. They figured out how to create a subscription service that complements their physical products, serving their existing customers' needs with cloud storage and more while creating recurring revenue.

The message:

Any business can do subscriptions with a suitable model.

It's just that selecting or creating the right model can be a little tricky, which is where this chapter comes in.

Here, we'll look at eight variations of the subscription model you may want to consider for your business. I will share examples of companies that use these models and provide a framework for choosing the one that works best for you. By the end of this chapter, you should know everything you need to know to pick the suitable model for your business.

Note: If you need some more support to choose which model works best for you, you can head to https://www.subscription-playbook.com to use my free subscription selector tool. Just answer a few easy questions and you will receive a personalized recommendation for which model could be best suited to your situation.

Let's kick things off with the subscription model that most of us are familiar with.

MODEL #1 – THE MEMBER BENEFITS MODEL

Look at what GoPro is doing with its subscription model. Members pay an annual fee and get many benefits they wouldn't have access to otherwise, including cloud storage, discounts, and editing tools.

That is the member benefits model.

Users pay a fee (monthly or annual) to get access to things non-members can't. In this case, those with a GoPro subscription can access tools that people who own a GoPro camera without a subscription can't use.

You can think of this as an umbrella model that takes bits and pieces of other models. For example, the software as a service model (more on this one later) offers benefits in exchange for membership. Only, in that case, the model is focused on software.

The member benefits model is more wide-ranging.

Why?

Because the benefits can be *anything*.

If you have an audience willing to pay a recurring fee for the thing you're offering as a benefit, you have the foundation of this subscription model in place.

Let's look at another example.

There used to be an Italian restaurant in Toronto called Grano. It was an exclusive place, offering high-end Italian cuisine to its clientele. But the brilliant minds behind the restaurant knew they could generate more revenue through a subscription.

How?

By hosting speeches from prominent people every year.

For $1,200 per year, Grano offered access to four private speeches annually. The restaurant, of course, was the venue for these events. So, not only did Grano collect subscription revenue, but it also profited from serving food and drinks during the events. And that's not even mentioning how these events can expand the restaurant's clientele.

Paying $1,200 yearly for some speeches might feel a little rich for your blood.

But as Grano proves, plenty of people value the exclusivity of these events enough to pay for them. All the restaurant needed to do was ensure the selected speakers were high-profile enough to make people want to pay such high fees to see them.

Sadly, the owner, Roberto Materlla, suffered a stroke a few years ago so Grano is no longer around.

Grano had a brilliant subscription business model, and I hope other venues can learn from and adapt it.

Again, we see the same model here as we saw with GoPro.

The business offers a benefit to consumers.

Consumers pay a membership fee to gain access to that exclusive benefit.

When considering this model, ask yourself if the benefit you can offer is substantial enough that people will pay a subscription for it *beyond* the main product you're selling them. Can you bundle additional benefits? If you can't, one of the other models in this chapter is likely a better choice for you.

MODEL #2 – THE CONSUMABLES MODEL

In the previous chapter, I mentioned I have a favorite brand of peppermint tea.

I told you I pay a monthly subscription to ensure a batch of tea lands on my doorstep every four weeks.

This is the consumables subscription model in a nutshell.

Your customers still pay a product's monthly (or annual) subscription. Only this time, the product is something they use and deplete. They will need to replace it, which is where the subscription comes in.

Peppermint tea doesn't last forever.

So, I pay a subscription to continue getting restocked.

We're seeing these models in all sorts of places. For example, Dollar Shave Club delivers disposable razors to subscribers every month. Amazon's Subscribe and Save program allows you to subscribe for all sorts of consumables.

But the one I want to focus on here is Vitable.

This company takes the consumable model a bit further than most. You complete a health and lifestyle assessment and, based on your results, get a recommendation about which vitamins you need to take every month to reach your goals.

Then, the offer: Vitable will deliver those same vitamins to your doorstep in a few days.

Its vitamin packs start at $1 per day, and you can customize your membership to have as many (or as few) packs delivered to your house each month as you want.

Of course, you're going to consume those packs eventually.

So, you set up a subscription to have more packs delivered as and when needed.

It's a brilliant model working in an underserved niche. And it's a model that has served Vitable well. It works so well that founders Ilyas Anane and Larah Loutati raised $5.5 million of funding in 2021.

What are we seeing with this model? Increased levels of convenience.

A subscription with delivery included means customers don't have to go to the store to buy whatever consumables they want.

We see the automation of a mundane task.

Picking up razors, buying tea, and grabbing vitamins are all mundane tasks. They're also easy to forget until you run out of the consumables. With a subscription, customers don't have to worry about running out.

And finally, we're seeing small businesses get into the seven and eight-figure value regions by offering consumables to their clients. If you offer a product that isn't particularly fun to shop for but could be considered essential for a particular market niche, you may have the foundation of a consumables subscription model.

MODEL #3 – THE UNLIMITED CONTENT MODEL

Another subscription model we're all super-familiar with is the unlimited content model, which probably did more than most to thrust subscriptions into the limelight.

Practically every streaming service operates under this model.

Netflix, Spotify, Amazon Prime, Disney+, Hulu, and so many more offer the same value proposition:

Pay a monthly fee, and we'll give you unlimited access to all of these movies/TV-shows/songs/whatever your poison is.

Who can resist?

Compare these unlimited models to what came before, where we'd often pay the equivalent of a monthly subscription fee just to buy one movie or album, and you're onto a winner here.

Of course, there's an obvious question to ask:

If you don't have access to thousands of movies or millions of songs, can you still make money with the unlimited content model?

Yes, you can.

The reason?

The "unlimited" bit doesn't necessarily refer to the content volume you can provide but the unfettered and unlimited access to it that your subscribers enjoy.

Let me hit you with another example.

The New Masters Academy offers a service to a specific niche.

Budding artists sign up for a subscription to take lessons from world-class artists. All the classes are in video format, and subscribers have unlimited access as soon as they start paying.

Now, you might ask how the platform managed to build up its library of content.

The owners bootstrapped it!

They got in touch with many prominent artists and shared their vision for what New Masters Academy could be. They then asked the artists if they'd be willing to record training videos—under one condition.

They wouldn't get paid upfront.

Instead, they'd receive a percentage of the revenue the website generates.

The gambit worked.

The platform has many videos and a reference library containing 35,000 high-quality images and 3D models. It has so much content that it can split membership into two tiers: $49 per month for Premium (access to everything) and $39 per month for Standard (no reference library).

A little ingenuity, and an understanding of what a niche wants, led to creating a successful unlimited content subscription service on a shoestring budget. Maybe you could take a similar approach. Or perhaps you're already churning out tons of content, and it's about time you monetized it.

Offer unlimited access to helpful content and you will find members.

MODEL #4 – SUBSCRIPTION BOXES

Certain products appeal to collectors. There are also product lines that provide so many options that consumers want a little help curating and finding stuff that works for them.

In either case, subscription boxes solve the problem.

The subscription box model involves recurring payments to provide customers with curated boxes full of a particular type of product (or products) that serve a specific niche. Loot Crate is an obvious example here. The company offers boxes full of T-shirts, figurines, comic books, and other memorabilia that appeal to the "geek" crowd.

There are plenty more.

Barkbox does the same thing for dog treats. Ipsy offers subscription boxes filled with new beauty products. And Stitchfix offers boxes filled with the latest fashions.

Then, you have companies operating at the market's premium level, such as Watch Gang.

Their model is simple.

You pay a subscription and get a new watch on your doorstep every month. The company collects personal details when you sign up to ensure they understand your taste. Then, it's just a case of waiting to see what you get.

Sounds simple enough, right?

Watch Gang made $15 million in 2017 using the subscription box model. It's now solidly entrenched as a top-level subscription business.

Why would a customer subscribe to this type of business?

The surprise element is pretty powerful here. There's something attractive about receiving a box in the mail that contains something you want. It's like getting a present at Christmas. You can't wait to open it and see what you've got. And a random subscriber wins a Rolex every Friday!

There are also savings to consider.

If you're running this model, you're ideally sending out thousands of the same boxes every month. That means you get to buy your products wholesale, leading to savings. Many subscription box companies pass these savings on to their customers. For example, some Watch Gang watches cost only a fifth of what they would at retail because of bulk buying.

And the company still generates a profit.

Ultimately, this model is about giving people stuff they like at prices below retail. As the business owner, you rely on bulk buying and wholesale to make it work. So, if you don't have a plan to achieve customer volume, this model may not be the right choice for you.

MODEL #5 – BUNDLED SERVICES

Also known as the "rundle," the bundled services model is simple:

Package together a bunch of services that people usually buy ad-hoc. Subscribers like the lower total cost and added convenience of knowing they have all these services purchased and paid for.

I see this model working well at the local level.

Take Lavelle Hairdressers as an example.

What do you mean you haven't heard of them?

Lavelle is a small hairdressing business based in Australia. Of course, it offers all the services you'd expect—style cuts, blow-dries, shampooing, and scalp massaging.

Each of these services is available individually with an appointment.

But Lavelle had the clever idea of packaging the four services into a subscription. Titled the Strength and Shine, it costs $64 per month. People who sign up get treatments they'd buy anyway. Only now, they get to save $108 every year with their subscription.

And therein lies the secret to making this model work.

There's little point in bundling services that people aren't already buying. If they don't like the service when it's sold individually, they will not fall in love with a bundle.

This model works when you have several services your customers use regularly.

In the case of Lavelle, the four services offered are all things customers will likely get during a single visit. To sweeten the deal, customers are allowed to add services to the four they receive if they'd like.

We also see many cable companies using this model. In the UK, Virgin and Sky offer TV, internet, home phone, and mobile packages—bundled together. Here, we see companies using attractive introductory offers to tie people into subscriptions that go up in price after a set period.

With the bundle, you provide limited choices to your customers.

However, you also give them related services they can feel good about. If you offer a set of services typically bought together, you may have the base ingredients for this model.

MODEL #6 – THE INSURANCE MODEL

Almost everybody has some form of insurance, so we know how the insurance subscription model works.

You pay a monthly premium to insure something—your home, your car, your life. In return, an insurance company guarantees that it will offer certain protections (and payments) should something happen.

We pay for peace of mind.

And it's a subscription model that has worked for decades. Insurers are some of the world's largest businesses because they have a recurring revenue model tied to something everybody needs.

These significant insurance subscriptions are perfect examples of a moat in action.

But what about the little guys? Is the insurance model just for significant players, or can smaller businesses get in on the action?

Smaller businesses can get involved because there are many ways to tweak this model.

Let's go back to GoPro.

When I talked about GoPro earlier, I didn't mention its subscription also gives customers access to an extended warranty. That's a form of insurance. End the subscription and you lose the warranty, meaning you lose peace of mind.

So, the insurance model can be tweaked to fit into other subscription models.

Then, we have companies like Babylon Health in the United Kingdom.

Dr. Ali Parsa founded Babylon in 2013 with the grand goal of making healthcare affordable for everybody globally. Babylon has yet to achieve that lofty ambition (the company operates primarily in London and Birmingham). However, it gives us a good idea of how a smaller business could leverage the insurance model.

Babylon gives you access to an app.

That app provides the "GP at Hand" service, which allows you to chat with a doctor and access their services 24/7. It comes with a bunch of little health tools too. But the constant access to a doctor or specialist is the selling point for the subscription.

Babylon charges £149 (approximately $200) per year for the service.

In return, customers get peace of mind. They know they can access a doctor at any time.

In a post-COVID-19 and increasingly remote world, it's a brilliant spin on the insurance model.

So, should you go this route?

Admittedly, the insurance model works as the primary model in very few industries. But even if you're not offering healthcare or a home service, you can still take elements of this model, as GoPro does, and integrate them into another.

The idea is simple.

If you have something that gives people peace of mind simply by having access to it, you have something that may work with the insurance model.

MODEL #7 – SOFTWARE AS A SERVICE

Again, we have a model that's familiar to most.

Software as a Service (SaaS) has been the dominant model in the software industry for several years. The general idea behind this model is that users pay a monthly fee for consistent access to a piece of software.

If the user stops paying, access to the software goes away.

Of course, that's a bare-bones description. SaaS offers advantages to customers because they gain accessibility features and access to consistent upgrades. They also get to spread the cost of using essential software over a monthly subscription, rather than forking out what would typically be a huge upfront fee for the software as a standalone.

So, who can we look to as a model for how SaaS should work?

The originators.

The pioneers.

Salesforce.

In truth, Salesforce may not have been the first business to attempt to use the SaaS model. But it's the first to get it right in such a significant way that it created the blueprint for every SaaS company that's followed.

Salesforce started as a Customer Relationship Management (CRM) system.

Before Salesforce came, companies that offered CRM software—such as SAP and Oracle—sold standalone products. They'd go in and install their CRM for you. And if you needed an update, you had to get the team in again to handle it.

That came at a massive upfront cost.

This meant many companies were operating with antiquated CRMs because they couldn't afford or weren't willing to spend money, having a company come in and conduct a costly upgrade.

Salesforce changed all of that.

The company put its flag in the ground early, offering cloud-based CRM services for a subscription fee. It told anybody who'd listen that they could get access to an excellent CRM in return for a low monthly subscription. And, ultimately, Salesforce succeeded in its quest to make it easier for people and businesses to access quality CRM software.

Salesforce established itself as the incumbent in its field, one of the essential elements of building a moat that we'll discuss later.

At the time of this writing, Salesforce is worth more than $200 billion.

It has consistently achieved revenue growth above 20 percent per year since 2013, with 2017 being a banner year at more than 50 percent growth.

Salesforce is the blueprint for SaaS.

It's the archetype.

And if you have software that has room to scale, evolve, and grow, you have the makings of a strong SaaS business. Just know you can't set up your SaaS product and then forget about it. You must commit to consistent updates and improvements to maintain loyalty in your customer base.

MODEL #8 – MINIMUM COMMITMENT

Minimum commitment adds a little twist to the subscription model.

In this case, you commit to buying a certain amount of a product or using a certain amount of service in exchange for a discount. We see this all the time in the energy industry. Suppliers commit to buying a certain amount of gas or electricity from producers. This gives the suppliers access to lower wholesale prices, allowing them to profit from reselling. The producer gets a recurring revenue stream that covers the costs of its infrastructure while enabling it to generate its profit.

A little closer to the type of business you may want to run, we have Stripe.

Stripe is a payment portal that annually processes billions of dollars of online transactions. A ton of e-commerce websites offer Stripe payments.

And that allows Stripe to run a minimum commitment model.

Once a vendor starts doing a reasonable number of e-commerce transactions, Stripe often makes an offer:

Commit to using Stripe for twelve months and you get a lower rate.

In other words, stick with us for the next year and we'll take less of your money!

The benefits on both sides are obvious. The vendor gets to keep more of the money its making due to the lower transaction fee. Stripe gets a vendor committed to it for twelve months. And because it knows that vendor is already processing a reasonable number of transactions, it will make good money for at least a year.

It's a simple idea.

It's also one of the many great ideas that has led to Stripe being a $100 billion-plus company.

Of course, there's room for this model in plenty of other industries. Data companies ask their customers to commit to buying a minimum amount of data. IT service desks often have minimum commitment contracts. And even reseller agreements tend to tie the reseller into hitting certain minimums.

This model works best when you have a product or service that becomes profitable at a set usage level. You want to make sure customers hit that usage level. Instead of offering standard use and hoping, have them commit to hitting the minimum. Ensure you can provide enough value to make tying themselves into such a contract worth it.

WHICH MODEL WORKS FOR YOU?

The answer comes down to the type of business you're running. What services and products do you offer? If you provide consumables, like my beloved peppermint tea, you have a model waiting for you. If you're a software developer (as I know a lot of you will be), the SaaS model works well, perhaps with elements of the insurance and minimum commitment model thrown in.

Ultimately, you need to figure out which models make the most sense for your business.

And if mixing and matching them makes sense, do it!

GoPro has already proven what works by mixing in a touch of the insurance model with the member benefits model.

The point is you need to know which subscription version you will use.

Once you know that, it's time to figure out your pricing model.

Remember: If you need some more support to choose which model works best for you, you can head to subscriptionplaybook.com to use my free subscription selector tool. Just answer a few easy questions, and you will receive a personalized recommendation for which model could be best suited to your situation.

CHAPTER THREE

CHOOSING YOUR PRICING MODEL

Figuring out a pricing model is the bane of many a company's existence.

Following a model that doesn't serve your business and, most importantly, doesn't gel with your customers can leave you down in the dirt before you know it. If your pricing doesn't hit home, that wide moat you've built won't help very much. Your competitors will have the chance to turn their pricing models into bridges they can use to cross your moat and break into your fortress!

Alternatively…

Potential customers will take one look at your pricing structure and walk away.

And when that happens, it doesn't matter how wide your moat is.

Nobody will be in your fortress, so you will have nothing to protect!

It's this exact situation that RapidSOS found itself in during its early days.

RapidSOS is an emergency technology startup with rural farm roots in Indiana. It builds "middleware," which means any software or mobile app can connect directly to 911 without needing to call.

For example, suppose any Uber rider or passenger feels they need emergency services. In that case, they can call 911 through Uber (using RapidSOS in the background), and the car make, model, and precise location is instantly sent to 911.

Today, RapidSOS is precisely where it wants to be. The company has raised hundreds of millions of dollars in investor funding. It processes more than 150 million emergencies annually (more on that in a minute), and 350 million devices are connected to its software.

And all that success came from a simple idea.

In 2012, Michael Martin, Matt Bozik, and Nick Horelick became fascinated with the emergency sector.

Why?

They looked at the numbers.

In the United States, 911 is the emergency phone number. That number receives 240 million calls annually. Those calls get routed to one of about 5,700 public safety answering points (PSAPs) around the country.

Each of these PSAPs is unique in its equipment and operational structure. They act independently, creating enormous diversity in the systems they use and the assets at their disposal.

But despite these differences, every single PSAP faced a common challenge.

Incorporating the information generated by billions of devices, such as GPS from mobiles and medical information from digital health profiles, into the 911 call process. With such an enormous amount of data available, how could these PSAPs find a way to sift through everything and provide first responders with what they need to handle emergencies?

That's the question RapidSOS' founders wanted to answer.

Michael Martin's interest in the emergency response sector was piqued by an incident he experienced while walking the streets of East Harlem. It was 1 a.m. when Martin noticed, out of the corner of his eye, that he was being followed.

He upped his pace.

The person following him did the same.

Martin crossed the street.

Again, this person followed him.

At that moment, Martin felt utterly vulnerable. What's more, he wasn't happy that the only solution to his problem seemed to be to get out his phone and fumble around to call somebody.

At the same time, his developing emergency had the potential to become more dangerous.

Thankfully, Martin walked away from the terrifying encounter unscathed.

And he did so with the seed of an idea planted in his head. This encounter told Martin a better way should exist for people to get help in an emergency. The concept for RapidSOS began to form in his mind.

At the time, Martin was studying at Harvard Business School. There he met Nick Horelick, a nuclear engineering student at MIT. The two hit it off and shared a passion for Martin's idea of improving emergency response. They linked up with another associate of Martin's, Matt Bozik, and got to work building a platform.

That was in 2013.

For the next couple of years, they worked on their idea. Their first breakthrough came when they figured out how to integrate a phone's GPS location into the legacy screens that 911 call takers use. That gave them a minimum viable product and acted as a proof of concept they could build upon.

As the team worked, Martin traveled the United States.

He visited PSAPs, spoke to 911 call handlers, and learned what the company's potential clients would need from the solution his team was working on. Martin created a spreadsheet and filled it with the information he gathered during his travels, holding nightly calls with the lab to communicate new ideas and iterations.

This process led to the formation of the company's government-focused platform. Better yet, Martin managed to get forty-four PSAPs in Texas to sign up as the first beta users of the new platform.

But there was a problem with this early model. The founders quickly realized they needed to move beyond local agencies if they were going to make any money from their work. And after deciding not to charge governments for using their software, the trio needed to develop some new ideas.

Still, they were in a good place.

They'd made inroads with the agencies that would most directly benefit from their platform. They had a minimum viable product established and a ton of feedback that let them iterate effectively. All they needed now was to figure out how to build more products that could use their platform to drive revenue.

They threw a few ideas around.

One of the early contenders was to sell their data to financial institutions. Perhaps the long-term plan could be to offer predictive analytics to insurance companies. After all, as Martin correctly pointed out, *"No one cares more about how fast the ambulance arrives than your life insurance company."*

The company even came up with a product idea—RapidSOS Predict.

Unfortunately, it didn't materialize.

Going back to the drawing board, the founders came up with an idea for an app called "Haven." It would allow a user to push a button and immediately send critical information, such as their location, to a 911 call handler.

It was simple, clever, and solved the problem Martin had experienced years before on the streets of East Harlem. It would get crucial information to a call handler without needing an extended conversation.

The idea started gaining traction.

Haven won many startup competitions, gaining about $500,000 in prize money. A Kickstarter campaign drew in another $60,000. The trio felt like they were onto a winner and launched a closed beta in December 2015. It went well enough to convince RapidSOS' founders to go for a full public launch in the middle of 2016.

Then the pricing problems started.

The idea was to offer a six-month free trial of the app, after which the user would pay $2.99 monthly. Martin assembled a marketing team that took to the streets of New York and handed out hundreds of business cards to get the word out. Martin was a part of that effort, securing a spot at the bottom of an escalator in New York's Grand Central Station. In his own words:

"I stood in Grand Central [Station in New York City] at the base of the escalator that comes up, where it's like a bottleneck, and I'm just

giving these cards to everyone. And I was like, 'Yeah! We're going to have a million users after today!' For two hours there, I'm just forcing these cards on people. So, I finally take the escalator up myself after I'd given them all out, and three-quarters of them are in the trash bin at the top of the escalator."

Those thrown-out business cards were a sign of what was to come.

People didn't want Haven.

They didn't like the idea of needing to download an app in case of emergencies. Compared to just dialling 911, Haven felt like too much of an ask. On top of that, people didn't see why they should pay $2.99 per month for a service they got for free when they dialled 911.

And so, we see a great app idea get shut down by a pricing model that didn't connect with the intended audience.

Of course, I've already given you the spoiler for this story.

RapidSOS changed its approach, choosing to develop technology allowing companies to connect their devices to the 911 response system. In the end, Haven was shut down in 2018, and its new business model led to RapidSOS becoming a massive success.

But I'm sharing this as a cautionary tale.

As you build your subscription business, you must pay close attention to your pricing model. Even a product that seems to offer a potentially life-saving benefit, as Haven did, can be rejected by your market if you don't nail the pricing.

That brings me to the topic we'll cover in this chapter.

You'll face some crucial pricing decisions that could make or break your business, so we'll examine five models for you to consider.

Note: If you need some more support to choose which pricing model works best for you, you can head to subscriptionplaybook.com to use my free pricing selector tool. Just answer a few easy questions, and you will receive a personalized recommendation for which pricing model could best suit your situation.

THE FIVE PRICING MODELS TO CONSIDER

By this point, you already know the pricing model I recommend for the subscription framework. It's in the name…

Subscription!

However, subscription isn't the only pricing model available to you. It's possible to mix and match the subscription pricing model with other models to create a more robust offering. I've settled on the five most applicable models.

Let's kick things off with the most obvious of the bunch.

MODEL #1 – REGULAR FIXED FEE SUBSCRIPTION

I know what you're thinking…

"Rob, you've already waxed lyrical about the subscription model. I know what it is. I know how it works. Do you need to go over it again here?"

My answer is yes—mostly because I want to show you that subscriptions can work in verticals you may never expect.

For example, the car industry.

Buying a car seems like a pretty cut-and-dried experience. You find one you like, put down your money, and drive away. Sometimes, you may take out financing or enter a monthly contract. But even then, you're essentially taking out a loan that eventually results in the car's ownership rather than engaging in a subscription that provides ongoing benefits.

It's a simple product purchase.

However, 2018 brought the first decline in private car ownership in history. And that happened partly because enterprising entrepreneurs are figuring out ways to turn car ownership into a subscription business.

Take Zipcar.

Founded in 2000, Zipcar allows users to pay a small sum ($7 per month) to reserve a vehicle they can access on-demand. It then charges the user an hourly rate for each drive on top of the monthly fee. It's a fantastic idea because it serves a market of people who want to have cars but don't tend to spend much time driving. Instead of paying huge sums for direct ownership, Zipcar customers pay a low subscription fee, plus a pay-as-you-go rate, to get a car only when they need it.

We're also seeing major car manufacturers test the subscription waters.

Jaguar offers their cars on subscription starting at around $1,000 per month—including registration, insurance, and maintenance. You can start, stop, or pause any time and get a fresh car every few months if you'd like. Car manufacturers see subscriptions as a way to drive additional revenue into their businesses.

Let's look at another industry: air travel.

Airlines have long offered membership subscriptions to get access to travel perks and lock-in with points to avoid using competitors. For example, the United Club membership gives you access to forty-five lounges worldwide and a range of other benefits for $650 per year. Not a bad deal if you can put up with their customer service (sorry United).

Jokes aside, the annual subscription fee has worked well for airlines for decades.

I could go on and on.

My main point is the regular fixed fee subscription model offers advantages for your business and its customers.

You enjoy a regular and predictable revenue stream that doesn't rely on one-time sales to prop it up. I've already talked about why the one-time model doesn't work, so I won't go deeper into this one. For your customers, subscriptions offer predictability in another way. They get to budget for a set monthly fee knowing they will receive a desirable service.

The simple fact is a subscription benefits everybody involved. Many examples I've shared demonstrate that it's a win-win pricing model. The only caveat is you need to offer something for which people are willing to pay a monthly fee. RapidSOS learned that with the Haven app. A subscription doesn't work if your customers can't see the benefit of paying a regular price for your service. They will leave in droves if you're not offering continuous and tangible benefits.

But when you have something that offers enough value to justify the recurring fee...

That's when you have a pricing model that supercharges a subscription business.

MODEL #2 – ADVERTISING

This model is simple.

Instead of having customers pay for your service, you bring in advertisers to pay for the exposure your service provides. You get a stream of revenue from the ads and build partnerships that may bring opportunities in the future. And your customers get their hands on whatever you're offering without paying a penny.

We see this all the time with mobile games.

Take PickCrafter as an example.

Developed by Fiveamp, the game used a fixed and rewarded video ad system. This form of advertising places control in the user's hands. Instead of interrupting play with random ads, the app offers in-game rewards for users choosing to click on the ad.

And it worked.

This non-disruptive approach grew PickCrafter's revenue by 165 percent. Engagement with ads rose by 94 percent too, which advertisers loved. And best of all, PickCrafter's customers got to play the game without getting interrupted every few minutes by ads they didn't want to see.

Of course, mobile is far from the only place you will see this strategy in action.

Go to almost any modern content website and you'll see ads scattered throughout your reading. *The New York Times*' website has ads in its sidebar. Yahoo! Finance builds them into its sidebar and header. And sites like Cracked and *Reader's Digest* will sprinkle ads into the content itself.

Podcasts often use the same approach.

You get the podcast for free, and the host gets revenue from ads sprinkled throughout.

YouTubers make money from in-video ads and sponsorships. The world's biggest YouTuber, PewDiePie, pulls in about $1.6 million *per month* from ads in his videos.

Social networks are packed full of ads, typically their primary revenue source. Email newsletters often contain ads, turning them into revenue streams and marketing tools.

I have plenty of experience with small businesses doing this.

One of my clients was a martial arts gym in the United States. My strategy for them was to partner with a bunch of local businesses to create a "Neighborhood Discount Card." The local businesses included a Domino's, a FedEx, and a bakery. The companies that signed up gave away special discounts to their customers. In return, they got featured on a flyer that every participating business placed on their front desk. So, each company got more exposure from being featured.

How could this strategy work for your business?

Let's say you run an SEO company.

That means all your services focus on marketing and websites. Perhaps you could shop your website around to companies in the web design and public relations industries. Your customers are likely to be interested in these services because they're related to what you do. That means these types of businesses can benefit from advertising on your website.

You build partnerships while pulling in revenue from an asset traditionally used to market your services.

So, we can see the advertising pricing model offers a ton of revenue-generating opportunities.

Unfortunately, there is a considerable caveat.

Advertising only works when what you're offering is popular enough to make placing an ad worthwhile for other companies.

Take YouTube videos as an example.

Sure, a content creator can use YouTube's in-built services to place ads on their videos. However, those ads won't generate much revenue, certainly not enough to sustain a business, unless the videos pull in millions of views. A video that only gets watched by a thousand people probably won't even make a dollar!

That holds for any service.

Podcasts nobody listens to won't attract advertisers. You won't earn money from content-based advertising platforms if nobody reads your blog. The simple fact is you need many people engaging with what you do to make advertising a viable strategy.

It's all in the numbers.

The more people you have, the more value you will get from the advertising pricing model.

Advertising can also be mixed and matched with subscription pricing. For example, charging a monthly fee for a specific advertising placement or reach.

MODEL #3 – E-COMMERCE

E-commerce is one of the world's fastest-growing models. It accounted for more than $4 *trillion* in sales in 2020 alone. And all the predictions only point to e-commerce growing bigger and bigger over time.

One of the many companies benefiting from this model is Catch.

Formerly Catch of the Day, Catch began life in 2006 as Australia's first "deal of the day" online retailer. The premise was simple. It started by showing one new deal on the site daily, and some of the early deals were quite remarkable. One day, it sold 2000 Asus laptops in a single hour. Another day, between 12 p.m. and 1 p.m., it sold $1.5 million worth of Samsung TVs (yes, in just one hour!).

Over time, the company evolved from offering a single deal daily to hosting more than two million products on its site. And in 2019, Catch Group announced the sale of the company to Wesfarmers for $230 million.

All of that was born out of a simple idea that caught fire.

Catch offers one of the more unique takes on e-commerce. In addition to selling products directly, it serves as an aggregator for other retailers, helping them make sales while taking a cut of the profits.

Catch also has a membership subscription called Club Catch. For $69/year, you get free shipping, exclusive deals, and discounts on insurance and cell phone plans. With more than 250,000 Club Catch members at the time of sale, it's been a great success. The company also reports that Club Catch members spend more in each basket and buy more often than non-members—a big win.

Wesfarmers has taken Club Catch to the next level since acquiring Catch. Club Catch is now rebranded as OnePass and also includes free delivery on eligible Kmart and Target items. If Wesfarmers adds its other retail brands to OnePass, it will be a serious competitive threat to Amazon in the Australian market.

And that brings us nicely to the giant elephant in the room.

Amazon.

You can't talk about e-commerce without talking about Amazon. It's the ruler of this domain and offers the perfect example of what can happen if you get e-commerce right. The company sells tons of its products on the Amazon platform. It also makes *billions* by opening its platform up to other retailers.

Amazon is the ultimate e-commerce business.

Scratch that....

Amazon is the ultimate moat.

Why? It combines every payment model I'll talk about in this chapter.

While e-commerce is its bread and butter, Amazon also offers the Prime subscription service, which rakes in billions per year.

Take a few minutes to browse Amazon and you'll also see many sponsored products, which means the company's making money from ads. And with their Amazon Web Services division, they're making money hand over fist from servers and other cloud offerings.

The e-commerce model is tried, tested, proven, and adaptable.

But it's also not perfect.

The biggest challenge with traditional e-commerce is it's often tied to the main problem I had with my marketing agency way back: one-off sales.

Assuming you don't build any other payment models into the traditional e-commerce model, you only make money when you sell a product. And once you've sold that product, there's no guarantee the customer will return and buy more from you. With traditional e-commerce, you don't get recurring revenue.

That's why you need to build in subscription pricing.

Look at LARQ. It sells self-cleaning water bottles and pitchers. You can buy the pitcher upfront and get replacement filters sent every two months on a subscription—a great blend of eCommerce and subscription.

In the previous chapter, we discussed e-commerce subscription boxes like Birchbox, Barkbox, and others that send you a monthly curated box. These are great examples of blending e-commerce and subscription pricing.

MODEL #4 – TRANSACTION PROCESSING

Escrow.com does precisely what its name suggests: It holds stuff in escrow for buyers and sellers, allowing them to conduct transactions flexibly.

For example, the owner of marijuana.com used Escrow.com to sell their domain. That was an exciting deal since the eventual buyer asked for terms that would allow them to pay for the domain name over *forty years*. So, Escrow.com is holding the marijuana.com domain name in escrow and collecting payments from the buyer to place in escrow. Eventually, the sale will get made.

Along the way, Escrow.com makes money from processing various payments.

And that is one example of the transaction processing model in action.

Transaction processing is all about being a facilitator. It's about helping customers get what they want and taking a little slice of the transaction each time.

Escrow.com's model involves holding other people's goods and money until a transaction is ready to be completed, at which point they release everything and take a slice for themselves.

The company has handled more than $1 billion in transactions since its founding.

Other examples of the transaction processing model come from the considerable number of payment processing platforms out there. PayPal is the most obvious one. If you use PayPal, you know it charges fees for transactions. If you receive $100 from a customer through PayPal, the platform will take a few dollars to facilitate the transaction.

Simple.

This model generated over $21.4 billion in revenue for PayPal in 2020.

The key challenge with the transaction processing model is that it's all about scale. You'll typically earn pennies on the dollar with each transaction, which means you need many transactions before making a profit.

Again, we can look at PayPal's numbers.

We know it generated about $21.4 billion in revenue in 2020.

However, according to Statista, PayPal processed transactions totalling $936 billion in the same year.

So, PayPal's pulling in more than 2 percent of its total transaction volume. And bear in mind, this is revenue—you've still got to account for overhead, taxes, and all of the other costs of running a business before you profit.

PayPal happens to have given us those figures for 2020. We know it made $4.2 billion in profit.

This emphasizes my point about scale when it comes to transaction processing. PayPal made only (and I'm using that term loosely) $4.2 billion in profit on transactions totalling almost $1 *trillion*.

You're going to need some deep pockets if you follow this model.

Your first few years in business will be all about investing and scaling. You'll burn cash until you get it to a point where it's handling enough transactions to turn a profit.

That could take *years*.

But that doesn't mean the model isn't viable. I just see it as something you build into another model rather than a model that forms the backbone of a small or medium-sized business.

For example, Amazon builds transaction processing into its e-commerce model by charging sellers a fee for every sale they make. eBay does the same thing and originally bought PayPal to double down on the transaction processing model!

Transaction processing can work. You just need *huge* numbers to make it viable.

MODEL #5 – DATA AND APIS

Data and APIs may sound like two models rolled into one. But you tend to find that companies that sell data also offer APIs, allowing other companies to integrate their platforms into their software suites.

Take RapidSOS as an example.

We've already talked about how that company struggled with a standard consumer subscription because of the nature of its service. It succeeded by developing an API that other tech companies could integrate into their services. That API enabled data exchanges, allowing RapidSOS to achieve its goal of helping emergency responders do what they do more efficiently.

With that in mind, how can we define the data model?

The simple answer is that data businesses sell...well...data. They'll usually sell it to other companies that hope to use that data to further their business ambitions.

Typically, data businesses sell their data as a service.

That means the customer can choose which data they need, pay only for what they use, and may even benefit from only having to make a limited commitment. Data companies sometimes even charge a monthly subscription (see how the models mix again?) to access their services.

Corelogic is a well-known company in the data game. It has collected an extensive database of historical and current property information. Corelogic sells this data for an annual fee to big businesses (banks, insurance companies, government) and even to individual property investors.

This way of doing business has been labelled DaaS, or data as a service.

The challenge is that having data doesn't mean anything if the data isn't helpful to potential buyers. With companies getting inundated with their own data, they don't want to purchase more unless they know it will help them reach their objectives. If your data doesn't fit the bill, nobody's buying it.

The regulatory issues around selling data compound that challenge. People get touchy about the idea of businesses selling their data to other businesses.

Frankly...

I do too!

The data payment model raises privacy concerns that you need to get comfortable with if you're going to use this model to generate a real profit. In addition to making the data you sell valuable and easy to use, you also have to make sure you're able to sell it without landing yourself in legal hot water.

YOU DON'T HAVE TO STICK TO ONE MODEL

I mentioned this earlier: Amazon is my idea of the ultimate subscription business. But the topic is worth covering again in a little more detail.

You don't have to stick to one payment model to have a successful business.

Amazon combines all five models I've discussed to generate revenue. Plenty of other great companies also use several of these models.

Consider Spotify.

Spotify leverages a freemium model in which free tier subscribers have to listen to ads in return for not paying a penny for streaming music. Spotify makes money from the ads, and the customer gets to listen for free.

Of course, we also know Spotify's primary source of recurring and consistent revenue comes from its paid subscriptions. It offers tiers for students, standard users, and even those in the same household to double up.

Subscription is the backbone of Spotify's payment model.

But it's making a ton of money by integrating an advertising payment model into its offering.

I'll repeat it:

You don't have to stick to one model.

You can often use one type of payment model to feed into another, which brings me to the next topic I want to cover.

SHOULD YOU GO FREEMIUM? – THE FACTORS TO CONSIDER

Spotify is an excellent example of the freemium model.

Free users must put up with ads for not paying any money to use the service. Those ads are obtrusive but necessary if Spotify is going to make any money from these free users.

That free subscription often serves as the gateway for paid subscribers. A new Spotify user may test out the service using the free tier, like what they see, not like putting up with ads or being unable to create their playlists, and sign up for a paid subscription to get a complete service.

That's just one example of freemium in action.

There are so many more.

If you've got kids, you probably know that Fortnite and its Battle Royale mode are the big things in gaming.

Fortnite operates a freemium model too.

The game is free to play and download. But if you want all the latest costumes, dances, and other cosmetics, you must pay money to get your hands on them. Of course, Fortnite also offers a subscription, Fortnite Crew, which gives subscribers a set amount of in-game currency, plus a few other perks, for a monthly fee.

So, we can see that the freemium model works.

It can be a solid gateway into the subscription model while providing a revenue stream as you work toward creating the recurring revenue you're shooting for in a subscription business.

But does that mean you should go the freemium route?

We'll need to dig a little deeper.

FREEMIUM VS FREE TRIALS

On the surface, freemium and free trials sound similar—but the reality is they're very different models.

With freemium, you're offering something for free permanently. While you may, and likely will push free customers toward a paid subscription, you'll also look to use other payment models to make money from your free membership tier.

Again, we have Spotify and its ads as an example here.

A free trial is much simpler.

You allow the customer to use your full service for free for a limited period. Once that period expires, they either stop using the service or start paying a subscription. Movie and TV streaming services use free trials all the time. Go to Netflix, Disney+, or almost any similar service, and you'll find you get a one-month free trial before you start paying for the service.

Both approaches can work.

Both can act as gateways into a subscription.

But which you use depends on two things:

1. Finding a balance between value and comfort
2. Your addressable market

I'll cover the second of these points a little later. For now, let's focus on the first.

When it comes to balance, you must consider what you're doing with the freemium model. You're offering customers a limited version of your service and a premium version, including all the bells and whistles designed to entice them.

Again, Spotify gives us a good example. Its Premium tier offers no ads, higher quality streaming, the ability to listen offline, and other valuable perks. This added value is designed to entice users into paying for a subscription. But its free tier still provides enough value to make it worthwhile for the customer. Users can still listen to plenty of music, with the limitations in place not being so massive that the service is useless.

And that's what I mean by balance.

With the freemium model, you need to offer a decent service for free while still packing your paid service with so much value that you can convert a decent percentage of your free customers to paid ones.

If you can't do that, which tends to happen when limiting your service compromises its quality, a free trial setup will probably work better for you. That way, you can offer customers everything for free for a limited time, giving them a chance to learn about the service and feel its value. Then, you rely on the service's strength, combined with your marketing efforts, to get paying customers.

The Addressable Market Conundrum

Jason Lemkin, co-founder of EchoSign, shared some interesting math on his blog that highlights the addressable market issue with the freemium model.

Let's say you're charging $10 per month for your subscription. Your goal is to grow the business to the point where you can launch an initial public offering, and for that to happen, you need to get to $100 million or more in annual revenue.

So, you need about a million subscribers.

That way, you generate about $10 million per month, getting you to $120 million per year.

But here's the catch.

The average freemium conversion rate sits at between 2 and 5 percent. If you go conservative and use the 2 percent conversion rate, you need a staggering *50 million* freemium customers.

The point?

You need a substantial addressable market to make freemium work. For one, your market must be big enough for you even to think about hitting viable numbers. And then, you have to offer a product that will snatch up a large enough portion of the market to hit your revenue targets.

Of course, you could always raise your prices if you have a small addressable market. But if that's your approach, you best be sure you can offer an appropriate level of value. If customers don't think they're getting a service worth the inflated price, they will stick with your free tier and never convert.

ANNUAL VS MONTHLY SUBSCRIPTIONS

The freemium model aims to get people to sign up for a recurring subscription. The same goes for the free trial model. So, our next question is, what type of subscription should you offer? Annual or monthly?

Each has its pros and cons.

Annual billing creates more certainty. You guarantee a twelve-month relationship with the customer, which gives you a chance to show that your service has long-term benefits. Churn is a lot easier to handle too. And frankly, it's easier for your business to collect one annual fee instead of twelve monthly ones.

But annual billing also means you're asking customers to put up more money and make a considerable commitment upfront. Many will feel wary about that, which means you miss out on customers.

Also, at the end of every twelve months, there is a big "renewal event" where you effectively ask customers if they want to renew. One of the best sales professionals I ever worked with referred to this event as "poking the bear." If the bear (customer) is happy with the service, why make them keep deciding to renew each year?

Monthly billing solves the commitment and big investment problems, which is why about 70 percent of subscription services go for monthly billing. The customer gets a manageable monthly fee they can work into their budget. And you may even find it's easier to showcase your service's value because you can attach a "lower" price to it.

The problem with monthly billing is customers can cancel on very short notice. Churn can become an issue, and you may struggle to keep customers on board long enough to recoup acquisition costs. Extra administration costs are also attached to tracking and processing monthly payments.

Your choice comes down to which option you think best suits your business.

Of course, some companies offer both, often giving a discount on the annual subscription because of the longer customer lifetime value. This approach lets your customers figure out what's best for them and ensures you don't alienate people who'd sign up if it wasn't for the considerable commitment you're asking for. But offering both creates more complexity in terms of your offer and admin work. So, again, it's something you have to think about in terms of what works best for your business.

Freemium or Free Trial?

Should you use a freemium or free trial model to acquire customers for your subscription business?

I'll summarize it with a simple table that tells you which conditions your business needs to meet to make each model viable.

FREEMIUM	FREE TRIAL
Enormous addressable market.	Small addressable market.
Your product is naturally shareable.	Your product is not naturally shareable.
You can offer enough value with the free version of your service to make it worthwhile while still offering plenty of value with your premium subscription.	You can't offer a free version of your service without stripping away everything that makes it desirable. Think Netflix offering a free tier that doesn't allow you to watch movies. Nobody wants that, hence the free trial.

In short, having a vast addressable market makes freemium viable. It may give you the fastest way to create the most significant potential audience, thus building your moat.

If you don't already have all of that going for you, the free trial approach may be best for you. You get to show customers what you have to offer without creating a scenario where most of them use the free version and never upgrade.

HOW TO CHOOSE YOUR PRICING MODEL

I've bombarded you with a lot of information in this chapter. And the sad truth is, I can't tell you the perfect combination of pricing models for your business. That's up to you.

But I can tell you two things about pricing.

First, no matter what models you use, the goal is to move customers toward subscriptions. You want that recurring revenue to create predictability and make your business more attractive.

Second, you've got to keep it low friction. Making your payment model confusing to customers just means that fewer of them will pay money for your service. An intelligent, low-friction pricing strategy can supercharge your growth and help you to build a wider moat. Sometimes the quality of your pricing strategy, if not the actual prices, can become part of the competitive advantage that widens your moat.

> **ACTION EXERCISE:**

Write down the pricing model that feels best for your company. Feel free to mix and match pricing models.

_____

_____

_____

_____

Remember: If you need some more support to choose which pricing model works best for you, you can head to the free resources page at https://www.subscriptionplaybook.com/resources to use my free pricing selector tool. Just answer a few easy questions, and you will receive a personalized recommendation for which pricing model could best suit your situation.

CHAPTER FOUR

USAGE-BASED PRICING: THE EMERGING PRICING MODEL

Procore is a leading provider of construction project management software. It's worth billions—and it has a strong value proposition on its pricing page:

"Explore unlimited plans for every builder and budget."

Sounds interesting, right?

If I were a builder or construction business owner, I'd like the idea of being able to add many people to my project management software. But at the same time, I'd figure there must be a catch. Indeed, there must be some limits to unlimited, right? How can a project management business give its customers carte blanche to add as many members to a project as they want while still offering a fixed monthly fee?

The answer is it can't! Or at least Procore doesn't.

THE UNUSUAL PRICING STRATEGY PROCORE USES TO SCALE REVENUE

Procore can offer unlimited users because it takes an unusual approach to pricing that we didn't cover in the previous chapter. Rather than having a range of fixed subscription tiers, Procore has a usage-based pricing model. It charges an annual fee based on the amount of construction you do each year, plus what features you want to access.

That means Procore prices its service based on the company using the service. No construction companies are the same, meaning no two will have the same project management requirements. This fair pricing model means small businesses pay less and big corporations pay more. It also benefits Procore because companies' fees increase as they grow.

By going for a customized pricing model based on usage, Procore attracts clients from both ends of the construction spectrum, with both small and large companies receiving value for their money. Of course, Procore makes more money from the large companies than it does from the small ones. But those large companies are the ones that take advantage of the "unlimited" aspects of Procore's offering—which means they're getting the bang they expect for their bucks.

And it's still a subscription because you're committing to a recurring annual fee based on your company size and selected features.

I find this usage-based pricing concept quite intriguing.

It's a twist on standard subscription model pricing and has potential as a model that could help you to widen your moat. After all, it allows you to tie your pricing directly to the amount of value that users are getting out of the service.

The more you give them, the more you earn. It's a win-win.

And if some recent company sales are any indication, the usage-based model is also attractive to investors. In 2020, Insight Partners reported on the IPOs of two companies, JFrog and Snowflake.

Both companies did exceptionally well.

JFrog launched with a share price of $44 and quickly grew to $64.79, where it stayed for quite a while. These numbers exceeded all estimates, which placed the company at a max of $37 per share. JFrog showcased 46 percent year-on-year revenue growth, with a net dollar retention (NDR) percentage of 139 percent.

THE MIRACLE OF NET DOLLAR RETENTION

As a sidenote, NDR is a metric companies use to represent revenue growth and churn over time from their existing pool of customers. The idea is to show revenue is rising from existing customers before any actions to attract new customers are accounted for. If your company has a high NDR, you know you are set for solid growth.

Note: In Chapter Nine, you will find a simple way to calculate NDR in your business.

Snowflake had a strong NDR, too—coming in at 158 percent. It also reached a valuation of $92 billion with its IPO and saw 121 percent year-on-year growth.

So, we have two companies that have attracted plenty of attention from investors and experienced phenomenal growth.

Guess what they have in common...

Usage-based pricing!

Both JFrog and Snowflake leverage the usage-based pricing model to achieve their growth. And after seeing numbers like the ones those companies achieved, I'd be remiss if I didn't dig into the model further. So, this chapter is dedicated to teaching you about usage-based pricing and what you need to do to make it part of a robust subscription business.

WHY ARE BUSINESSES FLOCKING TO USAGE-BASED PRICING?

The basic concept of usage-based pricing is simple enough. You charge your users based on how much of your service they consume. For example, Procore will charge customers that have a massive construction volume more than it'll charge customers that only have a small construction volume. Other companies may charge based on the number of API calls requested or active users.

If Netflix operated a usage-based pricing model, its prices would vary depending on how many movies and TV shows you watch. And that's a terrifying thought for me, given how easy it is to get lost in a Netflix binge.

You can think of usage-based pricing as being like a "pay-as-you-go" cell phone plan. Customers only pay for the exact amount of value they're getting out of the product. Businesses charge more to customers that use the service a lot while still attracting customers at the low end of the spectrum.

Now, I've mentioned that this is an emerging pricing model. Why do I say that?

On a small scale, usage-based pricing has always been possible. Again, we can refer to those pay-as-you-go cell phone plans. While the companies offering those plans are massive, the execution is simple. The customer has a dollar limit for the month. Once they reach that limit through calls and SMS messages, they can't use the phone until the next month.

Easy.

Usage-based pricing is a lot more complicated for software and technical subscription businesses. To make the model work, companies need to be able to track very detailed usage metrics, which means poring over a ton of data.

THREE KEY BENEFITS OF USAGE-BASED PRICING

There are three key benefits of usage-based pricing:

- Scaling Costs for Customers
- High Customer Retention
- A Wider Customer Base

Let's look at each of them.

Benefit #1 – Scaling Costs for Customers

Let's say you run a small construction company.

You're looking for a project management system, and Procore, which we looked at earlier, seems to fit the bill. However, you've only got a small team and are wary about paying through the nose for the service.

Procore's usage-based pricing is ideal for you.

Why?

It scales to the size of your business.

As a customer, you get to pay what you can afford to use the service. In other words, you're not paying for many bells and whistles that only become useful once your team has scaled to a certain point. You get what you need at a price you can afford. And as your company (and budget) grows, so will your platform usage. You'll end up paying more at that point. But you'll also be able to afford it!

Ultimately, usage-based pricing gives your customers more cost flexibility.

Benefit #2 – High Customer Retention

Sticking with the construction company example, we'll now assume your business has scaled to 100 people. You're using more of what Procore offers, and it's receiving more money from you. But that's okay because your business has scaled to the point where the extra amount you're paying allows you to receive the value and service you need.

Then, the economy tanks....

Or a global pandemic strikes....

Something happens that forces you to shrink the size of your construction business. Naturally, that also means you must reduce your usage of Procore.

But you don't have to stop using it. Just as Procore scaled up with you as you grew, it scales back down if you need to shrink.

Let's flip the script and take you out of the role of customer and into the part of a usage-based pricing model business owner.

That flexible scaling is terrific for you because it means you get to have high customer retention. Customers don't have to stop using your service because they can no longer afford it. Instead, they get to determine precisely how much service they use. You make less money from them than you used to, but at least they stick around instead of cancelling.

We see this in action with JFrog and Snowflake's NDR percentages. Those numbers are high because they're retaining customers who scale up their usage yearly. Still, they're bolstered by the fact that they also manage to keep customers that traditional subscription businesses might have lost.

Benefit #3 – A Wider Customer Base

I've touched on this one already, so I'll keep it brief.

Usage-based pricing allows you to appeal to customers at all levels in your niche. You make your service viable for start-ups, solo businesses, enterprise companies, and international businesses.

You get to invite everybody.

And that helps you achieve a low customer concentration, which builds a powerful moat.

POTENTIAL DOWNSIDES OF USAGE-BASED PRICING... AND HOW TO OVERCOME THEM

More customers, high retention rates, and benefits for customers. It all makes the usage-based model sound ideal, right?

Well, this model, like all pricing models, isn't perfect—you have to consider a few possible downsides, starting with a big one:

Less predictable revenue.

With a standard subscription, you set prices and know how many people are subscribed to each membership tier. If you have 350,000 people subscribed to a $15 membership, you can determine how much revenue you're generating by multiplying the numbers to get $5.25 million. Nice and simple.

With usage-based pricing, the revenue you generate varies from customer to customer. You'll struggle to achieve consistency in your revenue stream because you won't know from one month to the next if a big customer will cut their usage (or if a small customer will scale up). As a result, you may experience peaks and valleys in revenue.

For example, let's say that businesses in your industry slow down over the holidays. With set memberships, you collect the same money as always. With usage-based pricing, you get less because they're not using the service as much, so you hit a dip that (while foreseeable) forces you to adapt.

A while ago, I was the government national sales manager for a telecommunications company. We had a usage-based pricing model. One month, a government customer made a crazy number of conference calls during an election and spent a lot of money on our services. We celebrated! But then the next month, their spending dropped off a cliff and we panicked.

This example of "feast or famine" is a significant downside when we're looking to create predictable recurring revenue.

Next, we have the confusion this model can create for customers. When you have a set subscription, you have a simple offer: For X dollars per month or year, you get A, B, and C.

A customer can glance at the offer and know how much they're paying, what they're getting, and when they need to pay.

Usage-based pricing is more complicated to market. Sure, you can tell customers you'll charge them $0.001 per use—but it can be hard to figure out how much they will use the platform and whether your usage-based model makes sense for them.

That's why it is a good idea to bundle usage-based pricing with subscription to give your business more certainty.

TWO CLEVER WAYS TO MIX USAGE-BASED PRICING WITH SUBSCRIPTION

Usage-based pricing works best for businesses that can logically scale their offerings as customers grow.

Let's look at Leadfeeder.

The company offers high-quality leads to its clients on a subscription basis. At the time of writing, its pricing starts at $63 per month for up to 100 leads. It then increases based on leads provided, reaching $599 per month for between 3,001 and 5,000 leads. If you want more than 5,000, you have to get in touch to work out a suitable plan.

Usage-based pricing works for Leadfeeder because it can offer more leads for its significant clients while still being able to serve smaller ones. I especially like this model because it combines usage-based pricing with a monthly subscription.

ConvertKit, an email marketing provider, does something similar. In its case, the amount a customer pays changes based on the size of their email lists.

So, if you have a service that doesn't change, regardless of the customer's size, usage-based pricing probably won't work for you. But if your offer can scale with the customer, you may be able to leverage usage-based pricing.

THE FOUR FACTORS TO GETTING USAGE-BASED PRICING RIGHT

I see usage-based pricing as the natural evolution of the subscription model. It allows customers to start at a low cost and lets business owners monetize over time. It reduces friction, assuming you can get past the hurdle of explaining usage-based pricing.

We're not going to go 100 percent usage-based any time soon. Still, if you look at some of the prevailing trends in business (especially in the tech world), you see automation, artificial intelligence, and APIs coming to the fore. You'll see the continued growth of tools businesses can use to more accurately determine and predict usage, allowing for more accurate implementation of usage-based pricing.

We're heading in the usage-based direction—and if that's the direction you want to start walking in right now, there are four factors to keep in mind to make it work.

Factor #1 – Land and Expand

The usage-based model ties into the concept of land and expand.

You land small, offering a service the client can easily pay for. As that client scales, their needs expand. Your service expands to meet those needs, with your business generating more revenue from the client.

I'll be covering this concept more in the next chapter. The land and expand concept is why usage-based companies are so valuable now.

This ties into NDR, which we spoke about at the beginning of this chapter. High NDR is one of the reasons Snowflake and JFrog did so well with their IPOs. They landed their products with customers. Then, they expanded the revenue generated from those customers, leading to NDRs of more than 100 percent.

Factor #2 – Choose the Right Usage Metric

What primary metric should determine how much your customer pays for your service?

It's not an easy question to answer.

It must be a metric that grows consistently with your customers and helps you communicate the value of your service. It needs to be value-based, scalable, flexible, feasible, and predictable.

For example, Snowflake uses the volume of data a customer requires as its usage metric, which makes sense because it's a data platform. Attentive, which offers personalized SMS services, uses the number of messages sent as its usage metric. These metrics tie directly into services and pricing.

Your metric must do the same.

If it doesn't, you may base your pricing on a metric that stalls once the customer reaches a certain level. That means you give more of your service than you might intend.

Factor #3 – The Prediction Conundrum

I've already touched on this one.

Usage-based revenue is inherently less predictable than subscription-based revenue. Subscription revenue is fixed and easy to track—usage revenue changes monthly, based on your customers' actions.

The only way to counteract this unpredictability is to track consumption so you can make predictions based on data. This wouldn't have been possible a few years ago, especially for smaller businesses. However, with each new year bringing new advancements in AI (artificial intelligence) and automation, we see these powerful tools become more accessible.

Factor #4 – Proper Sales Compensation

Let's say you have two salespeople, whom we'll call John and Anna.

John made twenty-five sales last month.

Anna made five.

But Anna's sales are to businesses that are already a decent size. What's more, they have the potential to scale enormously in the coming years, meaning they'll also need to increase their usage of your service.

By contrast, John's sales are primarily made to small businesses that, while valuable, won't drive as much revenue.

Who should get more commission?

The answer is Anna, of course. She's brought in business that will result in more revenue for the company. But if you were to base your commission structure on the number of sales made, as you might with a traditional subscription model, John would come out on top. In that scenario, it would make sense since John sold twenty-five subscriptions at the same set price as the five Anna sold.

My point is that sales compensation gets a little more complicated with the usage-based model. To keep your salespeople motivated, you've got to reward them based on two factors:

1. The customer's usage at the point of sale because some businesses will use more of your service than others.
2. How that usage evolves. If the customer scales up, the salesperson should be rewarded appropriately.

Not accounting for usage in your commission structure will lead to a bunch of annoyed salespeople who eventually leave for greener pastures. Reward your people, and they'll return the favor with more sales!

THE EVOLUTION OF THE SUBSCRIPTION MODEL

I genuinely see usage-based pricing as the natural evolution of the subscription pricing model.

And for some businesses, the model is at a point where it's feasible. More prominent companies that have the resources to track usage accurately may be able to adopt this model. So will any business where the usage metric is simple enough to track without complicated tools.

But do I see this payment model working for smaller businesses? That's harder to answer.

The investment required to track usage accurately will outweigh the potential revenue benefits for some. You also lose predictability, which can sting a small business that may not be able to handle cash flow dips. You need to consider the model's upsides and downsides before deciding.

To close out the chapter, I will leave you with one important strategy.

You can turn a usage-based model into something closer to a subscription model by having customers sign a contract with a minimum commitment. For example, you could have the customer commit to a specific minimum usage volume each month or year.

This strategy works because you can set the minimum commitment to claw back the money you spent acquiring the customer. Then, you get to give the customer all the benefits of the usage-based model.

Now, I talked about the concept of land and expand in this chapter. That's a concept that deserves some further exploration, which is why we're covering it next.

ACTION EXERCISE:

Can you add usage-based pricing to your business model? If so, write down the details below.

_____

_____

_____

_____

If you would like to see some more examples of usage-based pricing, you can head to the free resources page at https://www.subscriptionplaybook.com/resources. There are screenshots and examples of companies doing usage-based pricing well.

CHAPTER FIVE

DIG YOUR MOAT: HOW TO PROTECT YOUR SUBSCRIPTION BUSINESS FROM COPYCATS

Nubank is an excellent example of a company that's managed to create a subscription business with a moat. It has grown from a startup bank in Brazil to being valued at $30 billion and attracting a $750 million investment check from Warren Buffet. All in eight years.

How? By completely disrupting the Brazilian banking sector and adding multiple moat elements.

HOW A STARTUP BANK COMPLETELY DISRUPTED THE BRAZILIAN BANKING SECTOR

Okay, so the Nubank story isn't quite that simple.

The company began in Brazil, a country riddled with contradictions within its banking sector. Despite being one of Latin

America's most profitable industries, Brazilian banking has enormous problems, ranging from terrible customer service to the utter failure to offer services to large portions of the country's population.

And then there are the interest rates.

An HBS study from December 2018 points out that the average corporate loan in Brazil comes with an interest rate of 52.3 percent. Consumer loans have an average rate of 120 percent. And if you have a credit card, you enjoy a whopping average of *272.42 percent.*

Those numbers are insane—and they are many multiples above what people in neighboring countries pay.

This paints a terrible picture of Brazil's banking industry. But it also reveals a massive disruption opportunity for a startup. If that startup could offer even the most basic modern banking facilities to an industry so poorly structured, that company would have a vast moat.

Enter Nubank.

Nubank was founded by a former investment advisor named David Velez. And the idea came after his employer, Sequoia, sent him to Brazil to search for deals, only to pull out of the country. Velez's search revealed that many companies looked like one another (especially in the banking sector), and very few had anything different or inspiring to offer.

In other words, there were many companies but very few moats.

Velez saw the opportunity.

If he could enter this industry with a subscription business that had a moat, he'd have a chance of succeeding. His own experiences bolstered these thoughts as a bank customer in Sao Paulo. Velez recalls that the process of opening a bank account made him feel like the bank was doing *him* a favor. Couple that with another experience: He was patted down by security, who thought he had a gun when his laptop set off metal detectors. It became clear that even a touch of modernity would make all the difference.

So, let's look at the key facts.

Brazil has a vast and profitable banking industry. It also has a population of more than 200 million people, creating a sizable customer base. Banking is a repeat service that people need throughout their lives. And Brazil had such low standards in terms of the quality of service its banks offered that a clear opportunity existed for improvement.

And Velez had one more ace up his sleeve.

Yes, Brazil's banking system could use a modern touch regarding service. But its underlying infrastructure is surprisingly modern. For example, the Central Bank of Brazil can process bank transfers at lightning speed. Granted, those transfers come with many fees. But comparing this speed to the several days it takes for bank transfers in America, Brazil's infrastructure had some advantages that Nubank could leverage.

There was a problem, however.

In 2013, when Nubank was founded and started attracting investment, Brazil didn't allow companies owned by non-natives to create banks. David Velez is not a native of Brazil. He didn't even speak Portuguese! So, if he were to revolutionize Brazilian banking from the customer's perspective, he would need to take a different route than starting his own bank.

So, Nubank created a credit card.

But this credit card was very different from any the Brazilian public had ever seen.

Those differences started with the branding, which used the same shade of purple you'll see if you ever catch an episode of *Barney & Friends*. People told Velez he was mad. They told him consumers would expect a more conservative color in their bank's branding.

But what those people didn't realize was the average consumer in Brazil was ready for something that went against the norm.

Velez then focused on making his company's credit card as accessible to the average Brazilian as possible. Credit offerings started from just $50 per month, making the card much more helpful in a country with a minimum wage of about $200 per month. The cards also came with no annual fees. Best of all, users can manage their cards and repayments via a convenient and *free* mobile app.

Nubank even created its own credit score, making the card even more accessible to those who either didn't have an existing bank account or were severely underserved by their current banking options.

In short, Nubank made credit cards more accessible than they'd ever been in Brazil. And this was shown in the stats, which revealed that 20 percent of Nubank's initial customers had *never had a credit card*.

Now, I could spend pages digging into everything Nubank has done to grow as a company since it launched its first credit card. However, I want to focus on this card because it offers an example of the subscription model.

The subscription aspect comes from the nature of credit cards. By using credit, customers tie themselves to a recurring revenue model as they repay what they've borrowed with interest. It's not a traditional subscription, but it is essentially the same concept.

Then, the moat.

Nubank's credit card was unlike anything Brazil had seen. It was branded differently. It made credit accessible. Everything Nubank's credit card did differently widened its moat and made its subscription offering even more appealing. And that is precisely what you want to do for your business.

In this chapter, I will dig deeper into building a moat for your subscription model. I will discuss the five strategic factors required to make this model work.

Think of this as the subscription-moat framework. If you get these strategic factors right, you can get the model working for your company.

MOATS—THE FIVE KEY FACTORS FOR PROTECTING YOUR SUBSCRIPTION CASTLE

Nubank is not the only example of a company with a powerful moat.

GoPro has one too.

It may surprise you to see GoPro mentioned here. At first glance, the hardware manufacturer seems to do the opposite of a subscription. GoPro builds mountable cameras that are durable enough to shoot video in the most extreme conditions. That's a competitive advantage, but it's not a subscription. Once somebody buys a GoPro, they're not obligated to give the company any more money. It's a one-off purchase.

But then, we throw the GoPro app into the equation, focusing on the subscription service.

HOW GOPRO ADDED LUCRATIVE SUBSCRIPTION REVENUE TO ITS CAMERA SALES

Using the app, GoPro owners can create short viral videos that are easy to share. With GoPro Subscription, the company integrated its app into a new service where users pay a monthly fee to get access to all of the following:

- Unlimited cloud-based storage for photos and video at 100 percent quality.
- Access to premium editing tools in the Quik app and an in-built soundtrack library they can use to add a little more oomph to videos.
- Access to exclusive offers, apparel, and hardware.
- Up to 50 percent off any accessories or mounts.
- Guaranteed camera replacement—subscribers can exchange up to two cameras a year. Basically like an unlimited extended warranty.
- A premium support service that helps them get the most out of their GoPro.

You know how razors and printers are sold upfront and people buy blades and toner over time? GoPro has done the same with cameras. You buy the camera and then have the ongoing subscription.

And just like that, you have a hardware manufacturer with a moat (the durability of the cameras) that has *widened* the moat with a subscription service.

My point in sharing this story is that even businesses that don't seem like they can leverage the subscription model can do it with a bit of ingenuity.

Your business can add a moat to the subscription model too. You just need to understand the five strategic factors that create a moat.

Those factors conveniently form the acronym MOATS:

- Marketing Supremacy
- One
- Audience
- Toughness
- Switching

And that's what I'm going to show you now. But I'd like to make a quick point before we begin.

Your company doesn't need to have *all* these strategic factors to create a business that successfully runs a subscription model. You do need to have *some* of them. And the more of them you have, the wider your moat.

So, let's kick things off with our first strategic factor…

M – MARKETING SUPREMACY

We can break down Marketing Supremacy into two elements:

- Acquiring Clients Without a High Marketing Spend
- Branding

Let's find out more about each element.

1 – Acquiring Clients Without a High Marketing Spend

The founder of Attention Grabbing Media, Manuel Suarez, is a digital marketer. Naturally, his agency offers services related to digital marketing. Recently, he started building Facebook

Messenger chatbots for online personalities that generate inexpensive leads. A chatbot is a computer program that simulates human conversation.

His business generates about $200,000 per month in recurring revenue. And it does this with Manuel spending barely anything on acquiring new clients.

How?

Through Facebook marketing, with a particular focus on Facebook Messenger. Messenger is a free service that allows people to interact directly with their friends and followers on Facebook. Manuel recognized this and used it as an opportunity to engage people. Through Messenger, he could build on the content he shared on his Facebook page into more direct chat experiences. This allowed him to start asking visitors questions:

- What is your current revenue?
- Do you have a YouTube channel?
- Do you have social media?
- How many staff members do you have?

All relevant data for the owner of a digital marketing agency. And all data that Manuel and his team could then use to dig deeper into his prospect's problems and increase his chances of making sales.

I'm simplifying Manuel's story somewhat, but I want to make the critical point that Messenger enabled him to attract clients while spending very little on his marketing.

And that is our first step to building a moat.

Messenger is far from the only strategy you can use to lower your marketing spend. Referral programs, investing in existing customer relationships, and incentive programs can reduce your spend. Understanding exactly who your target customer is and what they're looking for also lowers your spend since you're not wasting your budget on people who would never buy from you in the first place.

Not having to commit to spending millions on marketing every year makes a business extremely attractive to a buyer or investor.

Chapter Six covers how to grow client numbers on a shoestring budget. You can also refer to my previous book, *Feed A Starving Crowd,* for 227 free or inexpensive marketing strategies if you want to dive deeper.

2 – Branding

What do Booking.com, Google, and Apple all have in common?

Their brands are so powerful that they're the first port of call for anybody who wants the services they offer. Google is a perfect example. When we want to use a search engine to find something on the internet, we don't "search for it."

We "Google it."

That's a powerful brand.

Apple has similar power.

Most people who buy Apple products do so without comparison shopping. They don't look at the massive range of phones running the Android operating system. They don't research the stats and features of every comparable phone. If they did, they would find Apple sells phones for more than $1,000, with competing brands selling similar phones for a few hundred bucks.

They buy Apple because Apple is a brand with status. It has an element of luxury and prestige that most "regular" electronics companies just can't compete with. It also has deep embedding and switching costs, which we'll discuss later in this chapter.

There are plenty more examples.

Take Tesla.

When you think electric cars, you think Tesla. They've become the go-to name in that niche, to the point where people will assume you're going to buy a Tesla if you're buying an electric car. Of course, we've also seen other brands becoming synonymous with their products over the years—Xerox with photocopy machines, Kleenex with tissues, Band-Aid for medical bandages.

A company that has a strong brand—a brand people relate to and instantly gravitate toward—has achieved marketing supremacy. These brands don't even need to advertise their presence to consumers.

We know they exist. We know what we use them for. And we head to them in droves regardless of the other options available on the market.

If your brand isn't unique yet, don't worry.

A brand is one of the weaker moat elements compared to the others. Some companies with renowned brands have been thrown to the wayside. Look at Kodak with cameras, Yahoo! with search engines, Blockbuster with movies, and Borders with books. All powerful brands but unable to compete with stronger rivals.

There are plenty of great books on branding, so we won't explore this topic further in this book—but branding can help build your moat when used in conjunction with the other factors.

O - ONE

We have only one element for this strategic factor—No Single Point of Failure.

But I tell you, this is a big one.

The rule of one…

Listen to enough business coaches, especially those focused on startups, and you will see this rule. They'll tell you that you want one product, one target customer, one marketing strategy, one sales funnel, one….

You get the picture.

And the concept behind the rule of one seems to make sense. Having one of each makes running a business a lot easier. In the early days, it may even work out for you.

But eventually, the rule of one falls apart.

As you start working toward growing your business, you'll find that the rule of one limits your options. Even worse, the rule of one places a ton of risk on your shoulders. After all, what happens when your one thing doesn't work anymore?

We can ask Matt Mickiewicz.

Matt is a serial entrepreneur and the co-founder of Flippa, 99designs, Hired, and SitePoint. He's been there and seen it all when it comes to business. And in 2000, he discovered just how dangerous the rule of one could be with SitePoint.

He'd designed the business to sell ads and sponsorships online. This was during the days when pop-up ads were king, and online advertising was nowhere near as sophisticated (for better or worse) as it is today.

Then, the ad market dried up.

It seemed to happen overnight, and SitePoint's *one* source of revenue dried up almost instantly. Thankfully, the company could pivot to focus on selling membership subscriptions to end-users, meaning it managed to survive. But losing their one source of revenue very nearly killed them.

James Altucher has a similar story.

A hedge fund manager, author, and entrepreneur, James is famous for failing. Seventeen of the twenty-plus companies he's founded over the years have gone under. While this seems like it would make him a bad choice for business advice, James' history gives us some insight into the many mistakes and pitfalls that await a small business owner.

James' horror story involves losing $9 million in *one day*.

How did that happen?

His company's largest shareholder had to repay the IRS $90 million in back taxes. James didn't know this when he accepted the shareholder's investment. And the bank that loaned the shareholder the money naturally wanted to get its cash back as quickly as possible.

James lost his *one* major investor and had another failed company.

The point is you don't want just one of *anything*. To have a wide moat, you need to have multiples. Multiple revenue streams, multiple sources of traffic, multiple types of clients, and numerous team members who can do the same role. The only thing you need to know about the rule of one is it's the one rule you should break as a business owner.

I once had lunch with a well-known venture capitalist. He said he wouldn't invest in companies that were too reliant on Facebook or Google advertising. He had seen too many examples of businesses falling over while being at the mercy of these media giants.

ACTION EXERCISE:

Look at all the essential functions and key dependencies critical to the business. Think about sales, marketing, product and design, operations, customer success, engineering, suppliers, finance, investors, etc.

Are there any areas where you are exposed to the rule of one? Do you only have one quota-beating salesperson? One strong engineer? One supplier for a crucial part of the business?

If you identify any key risks, it's essential to look at how to overcome them. For example, maybe you need to hire an extra salesperson earlier than you want to mitigate the risk of your top performer leaving. If you only have one supplier and it is critical, can you shop around and get a second supplier as an insurance policy for a rainy day?

You can bet your bottom dollar that a rainy day will come. I once had a key supplier double its prices on me overnight, which destroyed our margins. It took six months to work through and secure a new supplier at our old rate. If I had that second supplier already in place, I could have saved six months of pain.

List your top five key risks and mitigation strategies below:

_____

_____

_____

A – AUDIENCE

We have three elements for this strategic factor to consider:

1. Low Customer Concentration
2. Network Effects and Shareability
3. Ongoing Usage

Let's start with:

1 – Low Customer Concentration

In 2015, researchers from Cornell University and Drexel University teamed up to run a conservatively named Customer Concentration and Cost Structure study. They aimed to determine how companies' cost structure decisions affected their future performance.

The study goes into great depth and is worth a read. It established a negative relationship between high customer concentration and cost elasticity. In other words, high customer concentration exposes a business to more risk.

What's customer concentration? Imagine you're running a business that produces engines for commercial airplanes.

Realistically, there are only two companies you can sell those engines to—Airbus and Boeing. A couple of other manufacturers could become clients, but they're nowhere near the size of these heavy hitters.

This is an example of having a high customer concentration.

Similarly, people get excited when they secure a big deal with Walmart or any other major retailer. They take a thin margin but sell more volume. The considerable risk is that one day Walmart deletes your product line, and you're stuck with hundreds of thousands, if not millions, worth of inventory you can't sell.

Don't get me wrong. I'm not saying don't deal with Walmart or go for big corporations—I love enterprise sales—just be cautious of the potential downside and think about how you can mitigate risk.

In this situation, most of your company's revenue comes from a small number of customers. And if one of those customers happens to go bankrupt or chooses another supplier, for whatever reason, you lose a massive chunk of your revenue.

This means you want to have a low customer concentration.

With low customer concentration, the loss of a single customer will not have a notable impact on the business. Netflix doesn't go into panic mode when John in Tampa cancels his subscription. Low customer concentration means your customer base is so spread out that you're protected should a customer, or even several customers, stop using your service.

Again, you're widening the moat by creating more robust defenses for your business.

A general rule of thumb here is that one client should not be more than 10 percent of your revenue, and your largest five clients should not be more than 25 percent.

> **ACTION EXERCISE:**

List your top five clients. Add up the revenue to see if it's more than 25 percent. If so, get to selling and sign up some other larger clients to balance this and reduce your concentration risk.

_____

_____

_____

_____

_____

2 – Network Effects and Shareability

In 2007, a YouTube user named Tay Zonday uploaded a video called "Chocolate Rain."

Maybe you've heard of it.

That video became a viral sensation—but for the first three months of its existence, nobody cared about it. The video only got a few views and seemed lost in the millions of other videos on YouTube.

But the video did have a small following.

A select group of YouTube users picked the video as ideal parody material, leading to a small offshoot of "Chocolate Rain" copycats putting up their own versions.

One day, YouTube decided to feature a bunch of these parodies, in addition to the original video, on its homepage.

The result?

"Chocolate Rain" has amassed more than 130 million views and more than 1.4 million engagements since April 2007.

This is an example of network effects in action.

Network effects means your product becomes more valuable as more people use it. In the case of "Chocolate Rain," the video became more valuable (and more beloved) as more people viewed it. The higher the view count climbed, the more people realized the video had value, which led to more people watching it.

Many companies leverage network effects today.

Take Udemy, for example.

Udemy is a platform for coaches to host and market their online courses. If you want to learn a skill online, Udemy is your first port of call. Its library has more than 150,000 courses and more than 50 million students.

My friend Shani Raja, a former *Wall Street Journal* editor, published some Udemy courses on exceptional writing. Currently, he has more than 460,000 students who have taken his courses. Who would have thought so many people would want to learn writing!

Successful instructors on the Udemy platform typically rely on network effects.

With network effects, an instructor's course increases in value as more people take it. When people engage with the course, leave reviews, and find it helpful, its value increases. Others can see that engagement and will be more likely to take the course.

The instructor then reaches a position where they can charge more for the course because the network effects at play have established that it has a high value.

In a sense, we can tie network effects into low customer concentration. The larger your customer base, the more likely it is to continue growing. The fact that so many people already use or buy what you're offering feeds into its value.

Network effects are so crucial that I've dedicated the next chapter to discussing them in greater detail—and providing action steps to get started with implementation.

3 – Ongoing Usage

You don't want to sell something once and have the customer never need it again.

For example, a doctor who cures an ear infection doesn't have ongoing usage because they've solved the problem. The patient doesn't need the service anymore, so they move on with their life, and the doctor loses the patient's business.

As part of the subscription model, we're looking for markets where customers repeatedly return.

Netflix is a fantastic example.

It employs a huge range of strategies to encourage ongoing usage of the platform. Its vast library of titles is the first strategy—having a massive selection of TV shows and movies means there's always something new for customers to watch.

Netflix builds on this by recommending content to its customers. Anybody using the platform knows it's constantly pushing you toward content it thinks you'll like, based on your previous viewing habits. So not only does Netflix offer a ton of variety, but it actively focuses on providing you with *more* of what you like.

The result? Extremely low churn.

As of the first quarter of 2021, Netflix's monthly churn rate stands at about 2.4 percent. The average monthly churn rate for other premium video-on-demand companies during the same period was 7 percent.

By ensuring its customers have reasons to keep coming back, Netflix maintains a churn rate of about one-third of that achieved by its nearest competitors.

And in an ideal world, your business will also give customers a reason to keep coming back. It's the capacity for ongoing usage that makes a subscription service so attractive to customers in the first place.

We are always looking at Daily Active Users (DAUs) and Monthly Active Users (MAUs) in the software world. In e-commerce and physical products, we look at transaction frequency—how often do people return and buy again?

ACTION EXERCISE:

How often do your customers either use or buy your products? Brainstorm three ways you can encourage your customers to come back more often.

_____

_____

_____

_____

T – TOUGHNESS

We have three elements for our fourth strategic factor:

1. Sustainable Competitive Advantage
2. High Gross Margin Levels
3. Marginal Profitability and Scale

Let's start with one of the most critical aspects of creating the toughness you'll need to widen the moat.

1 – Sustainable Competitive Advantage

Of all the elements related to building a moat, this one is second only to network effects. Your competitive advantage relates to your business' health, strength, and sustainability over the long term. The simple fact is that no competitive advantage means no sustainable business.

Plenty of examples exist of subscription businesses creating competitive advantages, but the one I want to focus on here is Peloton.

At first glance, Peleton's subscription exercise bike service doesn't seem to offer much beyond other one-time-transaction exercise bike companies. Sure, you get a workout app with the bike and can pay a monthly fee instead of buying it upfront. But apart from that, there doesn't seem to be much competitive advantage.

And yet, at the time of writing, Peloton has more than 7 million users and generates more than $4 billion per year.

How? Because *it does* have a competitive advantage…

Its members.

The secret sauce behind Peloton's success is the fantastic community the company has built around its service.

Peloton members can share their workouts with other people in their classes. They interact directly with other people using the bikes, which creates a sense of camaraderie. You also get built-in competition, which pushes people toward their fitness goals. And that extra push is enough to keep people around who might otherwise give up.

Of course, the community isn't Peloton's only competitive advantage—but it's the *main* advantage.

Peloton bikes are also built to a much higher standard than most other consumer exercise bikes. With Peloton, you get a studio-quality bike containing hundreds of in-built workouts. The company has also started widening its moat by introducing a fitness app, which is useful whether or not you have one of its bikes. The app contains workouts for yoga, Pilates, and even live classes with instructors while still providing plenty of content for Peloton bike owners.

All these things separate Peloton from the competition. And these competitive advantages lead to increased loyalty.

The company's churn rate stats bear that out.

Currently, Peloton has a minuscule 0.73 percent monthly churn rate. That's better than many enterprise software companies!

People stick with Peloton because of its unique community. And when you add network effects into the mix (a happy and growing community makes the service seem even more valuable), you have a competitive advantage that widens the moat.

Some "sunk cost" psychology is also at play here. Somebody who buys a Peloton bike commits to spending $2,000 on the equipment before transitioning to the monthly subscription model. They make a substantial investment just to become part of the Peloton community. And once they've made the initial investment, they'll keep paying the monthly fee because they don't want to waste the money they spent on the bike.

Of course, this is far from the only example of a competitive advantage I can share with you.

Companies like McDonald's and Walmart get ahead because of a cost leadership strategy. They offer products at the lowest prices, which draws customers. But I'm not keen on that strategy because it usually requires a massive upfront investment to attract colossal volume. That amount of capital is out of reach for most people. And if a well-funded competitor comes along and produces the same product for less, you don't have a fallback strategy.

In comparison, Coca-Cola and Pepsi have competitive advantages from their unique recipes. It's practically impossible for anybody to copy what they do precisely. So, they let their uniqueness attract customers.

And that's all a competitive advantage is: Something you can do that nobody else in your niche can do as well.

Where you find your competitive advantage is up to you. It could come from your product, community, how you serve customers, your operational setup, or any number of other places. The key is you have that thing that separates you from everybody else.

If you don't, your competitors won't even need a boat to cross your moat.

Important note: People can spend far too long focusing on competitors and get "analysis paralysis." I've always been a fan of understanding what competitors are doing, checking their activity occasionally, and then ignoring them and running my own race.

ACTION EXERCISE:

Draw a features matrix of yourself versus all your competitors. Then list your competitors' features and see how they compare to your offering. Remember, you don't have to be better at every single feature, especially if it's not valued that much by clients. Southwest Airlines was the cheapest airline with the best customer service, but it didn't offer seat allocation. Mailchimp was the first email platform to offer a free plan and focused on ease of use instead of too much customization.

An airline example is below.

	Southwest	Other airlines
Lowest fares	✓	✗
Friendliest service	✓	✗
Seat selection	✗	✓

2 – High Gross Margin Levels

Robust financials make a considerable difference in the MOATS model. If you can demonstrate a high gross profit margin, you have the attention of buyers and investors.

How do you come up with your percentage? A simple formula:

Gross Profit Margin = (Total Revenue – Cost of Goods Sold) Total Revenue x 100

Your gross margin matters because having a higher percentage means your business trades at a higher price/revenue multiple.

Consider Wisetech. They are a leading global provider of software solutions to the logistics industry. Their clients include giants like FedEx and DHL.

Wisetech's flagship product, CargoWise, has a 92 percent profit margin, with an exceptionally low *annual* churn rate of 1 percent. If an investor looks at those numbers, they're going to pick out Wisetech as a company they should get involved with.

Of course, Wisetech widens its moat because of the industry it's in. The company provides operating systems for global logistics firms, offering massive enterprise software programs. These software packages are mission-critical, costly to set up, and extremely hard to dislodge once they're in place (more on that in a moment).

Wisetech has the numbers. It has a product that widens its moat.

And it has achieved 1 percent or lower annual churn for the last *nine years*! Just to explain how powerful that is: If Wisetech had 100 clients at the start of the year, wholly ignored sales, and added no new clients the entire year, it would still have ninety-nine clients at the end of the year. An incredible business.

ACTION EXERCISE:

Calculate your gross margin. Is there anything you included that could be excluded? For example, Close.com is a successful CRM for startups, and it originally included unlimited free phone calls in its plans. After a while, it pulled this out, and the users had to pay per call in addition to the monthly plan.

3 – Marginal Profitability and Scale

Marginal profitability is another factor that investors will look at when determining whether they should pump money into a business. Marginal profitability shows how well a business scales. And you work it out by choosing a period, comparing it to a previous period, and figuring out the change in revenue against the change in costs.

You then calculate the difference between the two sets of numbers. If the new numbers are higher than the historical ones, then hey, presto! You have a business that's scaling.

For example, Microsoft has significant software development costs associated with building Microsoft Office. But because of cloud delivery, it costs Microsoft next to nothing when you buy a Microsoft Office subscription. It's all gross profit. Each incremental sales dollar requires little to no incremental cost since the development costs are fixed.

And scaling is good.

A lot of coaches and experts are now adopting this model. The traditional way of coaching was 1:1—each client gets an hour of your time each week. If you just want to work business hours, you are capped at around 30-40 clients max. A more scalable way to deliver the coaching is by creating pre-recorded videos explaining core concepts and holding a weekly group coaching call where people can ask questions about their specific situations. This lets you scale out the coaching to many more people, and your costs don't increase as you add more clients.

Of course, not scaling is problematic. And a business will see this reflected in its numbers. Take Google as an example. In 2011, the company posted negative marginal profitability in its first quarter results.

The company played it off, saying it wasn't worried about the numbers because it used the cash to invest in new ideas. And seeing how much Google has grown since 2011, it was probably telling the truth.

But investors were not happy about seeing negative marginal profitability. The day after Google's 2011 Q1 announcement, the stock price dropped by $48!

Building from marginal profitability, we have scaling. A company that has high marginal profitability can grow. And getting bigger is an advantage.

This is a concept called the "economies of scaling."

As you get bigger, you get more users. More users mean more substantial network effects. Plus, it usually means you can get lower prices from your suppliers—and possibly offer lower prices to customers, which means your conversion rates increase, and you get even more customers.

The numbers keep going up, and the business keeps getting stronger.

All sorts of examples exist of the economies of scale benefiting companies. Intel has intense competition in the tech world, for example. But its scale means it can invest billions of dollars into research and development. The scale of that development helps it remain a leader.

Amazon offers a prominent example of the economies of scale in action.

The more popular the platform gets, the more people buy from it. The more people buy from Amazon; the more sellers set up shop on the platform. And more sellers means more products, which means more money for Amazon, which leads to more investment in marketing and infrastructure, which leads to....

You get the picture.

ACTION EXERCISE:

Calculate how your costs scale as you increase sales. Ideally, your costs don't increase as fast as your revenue as you grow. Think of some strategies to serve your customers more efficiently through the scaling process.

_____

_____

_____

_____

S – SWITCHING

How easy is it for your customers to switch from your service? It should be as difficult as possible if you want a strong moat.

So, one element fits into this strategic factor: High Switching Costs.

Let's dig into it.

Also called embedding, the concept behind this is simple:

Integrate what you offer so deeply into the customer's infrastructure or life that they can't just replace you on a whim. Software is the most obvious example. You have an embedded product if you offer a software package platform that integrates with all the other software a company uses. To remove your software, a company must gut everything, starting from scratch to create a new solution.

TechnologyOne gives us an excellent example of this in practice. The company sells Enterprise software in big verticals, including government, healthcare, and education.

In 2020, the company's full-year results showed a churn rate of less than 1 percent.

Why?

Offering a quality product plays a part. But TechnologyOne's software solution becomes so embedded within organizations that switching costs are prohibitive. None of the company's customers will make the snap decision to switch. They'll see the price, rethink, and then talk to TechnologyOne's team if they have issues.

Those conversations allow TechnologyOne to fix any issue before the customer switches. So, the customer stays.

Plenty of other examples can be found of companies creating lock-in.

Gillette sells reusable razors. And customers need to replace the razor heads regularly to keep using their products. Of course, they can only replace them with Gillette's razor heads.

CRMs, such as Salesforce, secure their customers via the learning trap. Sure, you could go and install a new CRM. But even if you can deal with the cost of doing so, you must invest more time and money into migrating data and learning how to use your new CRM.

The most blatant examples come from companies that tie you into contracts for a set period and impose penalty fees for breaking them. Verizon and AT&T use this version of locking in. These fees are very unpopular with customers, so use this strategy cautiously!

The point is that making it difficult for a customer to switch, in whatever way you choose, widens your moat. It lowers your churn rate, allowing you to sustain your position and focus on growth.

ACTION EXERCISE:

Think through a few ways you can heighten switching costs. How can you become more valuable to your customers so it's harder to dislodge you? One strategy is to add more value and help with more problems. Another is to have a minimum contract length. Integrating and embedding with company systems is still another way to heighten switching costs. List a few ideas below.

_____

_____

_____

_____

TELL-TALE SIGNS OF A COMPANY WITH A MOAT

So, how do we tell if a company has a moat?

Looking for any of the strategic factors I've just highlighted will help. But for a public company, we're also going to check their financials over 5-10 years.

The numbers tell us everything.

If the company has had at least five years of consistent earnings, with share price growth, sales growth, and a consistently high gross margin, you could bet some moat elements are at play.

Why?

If a company can consistently grow earnings while maintaining high-profit margins, that tells you their competitors haven't been able to do anything to stop their growth. They've built a wide moat for competitors to cross, and it's hard to take on a company like that.

Stripe gives us a fantastic example of a company that has managed to build a powerful moat.

HOW STRIPE STARTED FROM SCRATCH AND BUILT A POWERFUL MOAT

Founded in 2010 by brothers Patrick and John Collison, Stripe had a simple mission: to make it easier for startups to accept payments online. The Collison brothers are smart cookies! At sixteen, Patrick received the forty-first Young Scientist of the Year award. John scored the highest-ever score by a student for the Irish Leaving Certificate. And before Patrick's last year of high school, he left early to attend MIT.

The brothers felt that the existing payment processing services of the time, PayPal being the big one, made accepting payments too hard.

So they came up with a simple alternative: A couple of lines of code that a user could copy and paste into their website.

And just like that, millions of new businesses had an easier way to accept payments. Stripe had a competitive advantage it could use to start widening its moat.

Since then, the company has introduced a wide range of other facilities. Stripe now offers capital, corporate cards, its Sigma custom reporting service, and Radar (its fraud and risk management service). All these services provide higher margins than the payment product they were founded on.

And higher margins mean an even wider moat.

We can keep going.

Stripe is more expensive to use than many of its competitors. While some count that as a point against Stripe, the company still has millions of users, despite the cost. Its focus on smaller clients, who prioritize ease of use ahead of price, plays into its favor here.

Stripe has a superior product for these users. So again, we see that competitive advantage coming into play. And because Stripe focuses on smaller users, it also has low customer concentration.

The company has some significant enterprise clients—Shopify, Salesforce, Google, Amazon, Zoom—but it also has *millions* of small customers that have integrated Stripe into their small websites.

Make no mistake; if Shopify left, Stripe wouldn't be happy. But its low customer concentration means it would survive and still have a base for growth.

Again, the moat widens.

This low customer concentration also means it can offer benefits to larger customers. Shopify pays less to use Stripe than Stripe's average user. The reason is Stripe knows it can boost its margins thanks to its smaller users. So, it can get away with offering lower prices to more significant customers because it knows it will make money back elsewhere.

The more significant customers get lower prices. That means they're unlikely to switch.

So, we see the cost of switching coming into play. For Shopify, moving to another payment processing company would mean it would have to pay more than it's paying Stripe right now.

That moat keeps getting wider. I'm showing you the tell-tale signs that a company has a moat.

But Stripe isn't perfect.

And this reinforces my point that you don't need *every* strategic factor in the MOATS framework to have a strong business.

For example, for a savvy small tech company, it's relatively easy for customers to switch to another payment processor. Most don't because they can't be bothered or don't want to waste time swapping processors, but it's not too difficult to do these days.

So, Stripe doesn't have the most substantial switching cost moat. However, I have noticed that as your volume increases, a Stripe representative will likely contact you and offer a better rate—if you sign a contract to stay on the platform for an agreed period.

Stripe also has limited international coverage. It currently allows businesses from about forty countries to accept payments, even though it will process payments from people in nearly 200 countries. This limits its reach when compared to competitors, which limits growth. But in this case, we can say Stripe has more potential for growth by expanding into more countries, so we could take this limitation two ways.

The limitation is either a sign that Stripe has a weakness, or it's a sign that Stripe still has the potential to become an even stronger company.

Then, we come back to margins.

And this is where things get a little tricky because Stripe is historically secretive about its gross profit margin. Stripe's standard structure is to charge 2.9 percent, plus a thirty-cent fee, for every successful transaction using the service. Stripe claims its margins are superior to those of industry peers.

Based on that, we can estimate its gross profit margin must be above 55 percent.

How do we know that?

According to a 2021 report by CB Insights, Adyen's profit margins are around 55 percent. Adyen is one of Stripe's leading competitors—and since Stripe claims to have industry-leading margins, we can assume they must be greater than 55 percent.

Again, another sign of a strong moat.

DOES YOUR BUSINESS FIT THE MOATS FRAMEWORK?

In Stripe, we see an example of a business with several strategic moat factors. It doesn't have all those factors in place. And frankly, your business doesn't need to either.

But having at least *some* of them provides you with a robust subscription business foundation. And with some of the strategic factors in place, you can start widening your moat to build an even stronger company.

> **ACTION EXERCISE:**

Go through the five strategic MOATS factors and analyze your current business against them. Give yourself a score out of five for each of the factors. For any aspects where you score low, consider whether there are any elements you can apply to your business. Don't worry if you can't think of all the answers now; the rest of the book contains examples and exercises to help stimulate your thinking.

_____

_____

_____

_____

_____

Note: If you would like a more detailed scorecard of how your business ranks against the MOATS factors, head to subscriptionplaybook.com/resources where you can use the free diagnostic tool.

CHAPTER SIX

NETWORK EFFECTS: THE LITTLE-KNOWN STRATEGY TURNING SMALL COMPANIES INTO FORTRESSES

We touched on network effects in Chapter Five. You already know the basic concept—a product or service becomes more valuable as more people use it.

What I haven't told you yet is that network effects can be your company's secret weapon. I'd even go so far as to say it's this strategy, more than any other, that allows small businesses to build the mighty fortresses their subscriptions guard. And I have the perfect example of network effects in action.

HOW PETE AND SAMI TRANSFORMED THE REAL ESTATE INDUSTRY AND EXITED FOR $3.5B

In 2005, Pete Flint and Sami Inkinen founded an online real estate marketplace called Trulia.

The idea came to Pete in 2004, when he was still a fresh-faced Stanford graduate. Arriving in Silicon Valley, Pete couldn't help but notice everybody around him seemed swept up in Google's IPO that year. But that wasn't the only thing on Pete's mind.

He was new to Silicon Valley, so he needed to find somewhere to live. He expected somebody to have already created an online tool to help him, so he jumped online to search.

Pete found nothing.

Frustrated, he kept searching for a house while attending conferences. One day, he found himself sitting in the back of a real estate conference in San Francisco. And that's when it hit him. Based on what he saw at the conference, it was clear the real estate industry struggled to adapt to new technology.

The industry was still spending *billions* of dollars on offline advertising.

What if he could create an online tool to allow real estate companies to showcase their properties? And even better, what if that tool would enable buyers to search through properties the way he'd so desperately wanted to do?

The idea for Trulia was born.

Pete knew his idea had potential. However, he also knew he had a problem to confront.

A pair of them!

He had a "chicken and egg" situation on his hands. How could he attract real estate listings with a service that didn't have an audience? And how could he attract an audience if he didn't have any real estate listings to show them?

It's a dilemma that can make your head spin—and the solution was to create a marketplace network effect that would bring buyers and agents together.

Pete and his team started speaking to brokers and asking for access to their data feeds. Most brokers didn't have a feed to access, so the team built a search engine dedicated to real estate. The brokers and agents Pete spoke to could index their listings in the search engine. The Trulia team started gaining snippets of information that helped them build the supply side of their business. And the agents benefited because this new search engine sent traffic to their websites.

It was complicated and required a lot of legwork.

But soon, the agents who chose to work with Pete started seeing the benefits. As they indexed more listings with the search engine, more potential buyers started using Trulia. This led to more inquiries to the agents, resulting in Trulia indexing more properties. More properties meant more users. Over time, other agents and brokers started seeing the benefits of indexing their listings with Trulia. So, they jumped onboard. And as the supply side of the business kept growing, so did the user-base of buyers.

That is network effects in action.

By building the tool and bringing it directly to a market segment, Pete and his team could get the wheels moving on their idea. And once those wheels were moving, the momentum kept building, and Trulia became an even more robust search engine.

This is just one aspect of network effects that Trulia used to become one of the world's foremost property search engines. Eventually, the business grew to such a size that Pete was able to sell it to Zillow in a transaction valued at $3.5 billion.

And it all started with a search engine and some direct work with real estate agents.

There is more to the Trulia story and its use of network effects that I don't have the space to cover in this book. Here, I'm just looking to showcase how network effects can help even the smallest of businesses build momentum and drive growth that puts them in the multi-billion-dollar value category.

Sounds good, right? Network effects are the secret weapon.

And in this chapter, we're going to dig into the six types of network effects you can leverage, as well as a few other ideas to help your network effects stretch even further.

NETWORK EFFECTS ARE ALL AROUND US

I've already given you the basic idea of what network effects are.

The simple answer to this question is that network effects are when a company's service becomes more valuable as usage increases. This is what we saw with Trulia. Once potential buyers started using the search engine, real estate agents began getting more inquiries. Those additional inquiries encouraged them to list more properties. More users followed, which created more value, and....

The rest is history.

The same concept happened with YouTube.

YouTube would not be the multi-billion-dollar monolith it is today if people didn't upload videos to the platform. User-generated content is its entire business model. The good news for the platform is that millions of people upload content. The more videos that get uploaded, the more people watch them. With more people watching, content creators have an incentive to keep creating. That means more videos, which leads to more views, and...

Again, you get the picture!

You are in a powerful position if you can find a way to add network effects to your subscription business. If you were to put me on the spot and ask me to choose just one of the subscription factors from previous chapters to use, I'd go for network effects.

It's the strategic factor that seven of the world's top ten companies use. Apple, Microsoft, Google, Amazon, Tencent, Alibaba, and Facebook all rely on network effects to some extent. And with this chapter's help, you'll see how your business can do the same thing.

THE SIX MAJOR TYPES OF NETWORK EFFECTS

In the Trulia story, we saw marketplace network effects in action. But that's just one of several types of network effects your business may be able to leverage.

I could probably spend an entire book exploring the many types of network effects out there. If you want to dive deeper, NFX (a venture capital firm) has a great blog.

But to keep things simple, I'm going to pick out the six I think are both the most powerful and the most likely to apply to the largest selection of business types. Let's kick things off with…

Network Effect #1 – The Industry Standard

The industry standard is inescapable—it's embedded in all products and related workflows.

Ultimately, you can think of the industry standard as a "universal" process, method, or product that applies to everybody in that process, method, or product's industry. And to get to that point, you need to establish a product or service that is indispensable to a niche market.

That's what the Real Estate Institute of New South Wales (REINSW) in Australia did.

Currently, more than 5,000 real estate agencies are operating in Sydney alone. Step outside Sydney and you can add thousands more to that list. Years ago, every one of those agencies had its own forms and agreement documents.

The real estate industry had no set standard.

Then, REINSW came along.

The organization became the advocacy group for real estate agents. It also created standardized forms and documents that many agents use today. Granted, the business may not be known internationally. Still, it has established its services as the industry standard in its niche—meaning it will be nearly impossible for any similar organization to replace it.

So, this leads us to a question...

Is there anything your business does, or offers, that could become the standard for your industry? If so, you have the potential to leverage this type of network effect.

But there's one little ingredient you need to add to the industry-standard network effect to make it take off:

Expertise.

If your product or service is backed by industry expertise and helps experts within your industry do their jobs, you have some powerful network effects.

Again, I can point you to REINSW.

Some local real estate experts founded the organization. Those experts develop its products and services for other experts. The tools it produces require real estate expertise to use. And the need for that expertise embeds those tools further into the NSW real estate niche, creating an even more powerful industry-standard network effect.

Give people something so good that they can't envision using anything else, and you have an industry standard. Back it up with expertise, perhaps even to the point where what you offer requires expertise to use, and you're just digging that moat even deeper!

Network Effect #2 – Media, Content, Messaging

Attention is valuable.

The more eyes you can bring to something, the more people (particularly advertisers) will pay attention to it. This is something we've seen for decades in the world of television. Shows with higher ratings attract advertisers willing to pay more to get their ads slotted into the show.

The network makes more money. The writers and actors make more money. And that all comes from the enormous amount of attention the show captures.

We see two layers in action with the media, content, and messaging network effect.

1. The "content marketplace." In this layer, content is supply, and attention is demand. More content leads to more attention, which then leads to:
2. Messaging or advertising.

If the supply of content draws enough attention, advertisers will come calling. Interestingly, this is where we see a switch in supply and demand dynamics. For advertisers, the supply does not come from the content. It comes from the people paying attention to that content. The more people pay attention, the more demand there will be from advertisers to associate their messages with the content.

Think of this as a three-sided marketplace.

As mentioned, we've seen this for years on TV. But I can point to plenty more. YouTube thrives on this version of network effects. Social media does too, as any social media platform becomes more valuable when its content leads to more users, which leads to more advertising.

Netflix and Disney+ use this form of network effects. Only in their cases, the content supply attracts attention that they convert into subscription billing.

And that's where this form of network effects becomes relevant to our subscription business. You can then monetize if you can create novel and exciting content—be it text, video, games, or whatever—you attract attention.

The Urban Developer in Australia gives us a great example of a smaller business using this network effect. The company is a small team of twelve people curating the most important news stories from Australia's property development sector.

Those stories attract attention.

That attention has led to relevant brands wanting to work with the company. Today, the Urban Developer generates a solid revenue stream by linking its readers with the brands they have attracted.

And that's not all...

The attention it gained through curating content has allowed the company to set up a subscription service called TUD+. Sign up, and you get access to exclusive content and webinars that you don't get via the base website. That's another revenue stream—a recurring one at that.

And so, we see how the media, content, and messaging network effect turns attention into profit potential.

Network Effect #3 – Marketplaces

Now let's return to the network effect that Trulia did such an excellent job of leveraging.

Marketplaces are a great business model because you can start quickly by focusing on a localized micro-niche. That's what the team at Trulia did. When first developing their real estate search engine, they weren't traveling the length and breadth of the

United States to get agents to allow them to index their properties. They stuck to Silicon Valley and the surrounding areas.

They started small, got listings indexed, began attracting buyers, and built from there.

It seems like there are marketplaces for everything these days! And marketplaces are commoditizing previously highly specialized skill sets. For example, there are now websites where you can book an instant consultation with a doctor, literally 24/7. I just checked, and you can book in fifteen-minute intervals starting now. You can book a session at precisely 3:45 a.m. if you'd like.

You could spin something like this up for a ton of different services. For example, you could start a marketplace like Uber for physiotherapists in your local area. Approach a bunch of physiotherapists who would like more work, hire an app developer to build a simple first version of the app, and run some Facebook and Google ads to get the word out to consumers. Then you can add subscription billing to get discounted monthly visits.

Marketplaces are unique because they bring buyers and sellers together. The more sellers a platform has, the more buyers get drawn to it. More sellers want to join when more buyers are on the platform because they can sniff out the profit potential.

More sellers lead to more buyers, and so on. Again, it's precisely what we saw with Trulia.

And with this network effect, you create a more defensible business. Buyers and sellers use the platform because other buyers and sellers use it. Of course, Trulia is far from the only example of this network effect in action.

Take eBay as another.

Anybody could build an auction website that works in much the same way as eBay. However, eBay is the known brand with a vast number of sellers. Those sellers offer so many items that they naturally attract more buyers. More buyers means more sellers, and now I feel like I'm starting to repeat myself!

Realestate.com.au is another excellent example.

That website has been Australia's leading property listing portal for more than two decades. It generated $1 billion of revenue in 2021, with a 92 percent gross margin and 47 percent operating margin. It is another incredible (and highly defensible) business.

If you need proof of that, there's a figurative graveyard filled with the businesses that have tried to do what Realestate.com.au does. None succeeded because it's almost impossible to unseat an incumbent marketplace. Again, refer to eBay and how it is still the world's dominant online auction site after more than twenty years. The only way to disrupt these monster businesses is to build a better experience for buyers and sellers simultaneously. Otherwise, nobody will change platforms.

Unfortunately, this form of network effect isn't perfect.

Attracting more buyers and sellers to a platform has downsides because it creates competition. Some frustrated buyers and sellers may move on because they can't establish a foothold on a platform. But typically, the number of people who move on is far outweighed by those who stick around.

More concerning is the concept of multi-tenanting.

Though I've highlighted eBay as the leading example of an online auction website, it still has to deal with multi-tenanting. This happens when nothing stops a seller from listing their product on multiple platforms. In the case of eBay, a seller could also list their products on Etsy, Amazon, and any other online platform. So, the marketplace network effect gets diluted.

Overcoming this drawback is a little more complicated.

It's hard to lock out competition from similar platforms when there is no penalty for using them. The only solution is to create so much value, particularly on the supply (or seller) side, that members aren't tempted to multi-tenant. That value can come from the marketing tools you offer and the higher volume of buyers on your platform.

To create that value, eBay is pushing to offer more value to its suppliers with its eBay Stores membership. Sellers who subscribe get more tools and benefits, and eBay gets to provide the value that dissuades multi-tenanting while collecting subscription income.

Win-win!

So, we can see that the marketplaces network effect can lead to massive success despite having its downsides. Now, there's one more cautionary tale I'd like to share before we move on to our following network effect.

It involves a guy named Ethan Stock.

He was living the Silicon Valley dream. He'd created a company that he sold to eBay for a ton of money. Ethan was a success by any person's definition of the word. But it hadn't always been like that.

Once upon a time, Ethan had owned a business called Zvents. He grew the company into the largest events site of its kind using marketplace network effects. Event holders listed their events for 14 million monthly users to see. And with new users pulling in more event organizers, everything seemed to be going well.

The problem was that Ethan wasn't getting paid. And this, as he explains, was all due to one issue in his model:

"There is a fatal flaw in some marketplace businesses that can hogtie their ability to make money—the expectation of completeness."

Ethan's plan had always been to grow the business to the point where he could feel comfortable asking event organizers to pay for their listings. To do that, he needed to attract enough visitors to make the payment worth it. But every Zvents visitor expected a complete and comprehensive listing of all of the events in their local area. So, Ethan had to provide completeness to attract visitors—meaning, he was left with a Catch-22 situation.

When he asked event organizers to pay for their listings, they all said, "What for?"

And Ethan was stuck.

He couldn't remove the listings. If he did, the visitors wouldn't come anymore. And if the visitors didn't come, he'd lose the leverage that would allow him to ask for payment in the first place.

Ultimately, Ethan couldn't develop a way to make Zvents profitable for himself. And therein lies our lesson about the marketplace network effect:

It's only effective if you can find a way to make sure you're getting paid.

One option is to facilitate transactions on your platform, as Uber and Upwork do. Another is, as eBay does, to take a slice out of a sale. Bark, a services marketplace, charges a cost per inquiry to the service professional. Just make sure you've found a way to monetize early on, or you may find your business ends up growing without ever generating a profit.

Network Effect #4 – Platforms

This type of network effect is similar to marketplaces but with one key difference: It only allows you to supply available products on the platform.

We see this all of the time in the video game industry. Consider the battle between Nintendo, Sony, and Microsoft. Here we have companies producing hardware that costs anywhere from $300 to $500. Buying all three platforms is cost-prohibitive for most gamers. So, each platform has to develop ways to draw people in.

How? By offering exclusive software that can't be found on any other platform.

We have the Halo and Gears of War games for Microsoft's Xbox consoles. Sony has games like *The Last of Us* and *Uncharted*. Nintendo produces *Mario*, *Metroid*, and *Legend of Zelda* for its platform. As a gamer, you can't find these exclusive titles anywhere else. So, you buy the platform that offers the most appealing content.

The console manufacturers dig deeper into this by tying developers to their platforms with exclusivity deals. And what we see happen is communities forming around each platform. On a very general level, Sony is where you go for story-driven exclusive experiences. If you want high-quality action games, off you go to Microsoft. But if it's a traditional, Disney-esque experience you're looking for, Nintendo is where you want to be.

I'm simplifying the platform effect a little here.

Each of these consoles also has hardware features that set them apart and subscription services—such as Game Pass or PS Now—that tie further into the platform network effect.

But the critical point here is that exclusivity to a platform creates community, leading to a network effect.

Many software companies are also going down this platform path. If you look at CRMs, they usually have an "App Store" of sorts with third-party add-ons you can buy. Most Smart TVs now have an app store too. Autodesk has the "Autodesk Developer Network," a community of developers who build additional functionality for their products.

Even smaller businesses have long-held preferred partner lists or affiliate networks of companies they work well with. A wedding planner has relationships with dressmakers, venues, and photographers. A general practitioner doctor has a team of specialists they work with. When I ran my marketing agency, I was the "platform" for all of my clients' marketing needs and plugged in whatever "add-on" the particular client needed. For example, if they had a lot of web traffic but a lousy website, I'd connect them with my preferred web designer and manage the process.

Platforms are nothing new, but software and gaming companies have put a new spin on things.

Again, like marketplaces, platforms aren't perfect. There's still potential for people to multi-tenant, but it happens less than in marketplaces.

Network Effect #5 – Data

This network effect occurs when a product's value increases as the product gathers more data. Moreover, the network effect compounds if continued product usage yields even more data. Ultimately, the data becomes the source of value and, in a subscription business, the reason somebody may choose to use or subscribe to a service.

Let's look at Waze.

On the surface, this is a simple mobile app that gives users driving directions.

But underneath the surface, you have an app constantly collecting traffic conditions data in real-time. That's where the strength of the business comes from. Nobody cares about yesterday's traffic. That's old news. They care about what traffic is like *right now*. By collecting that data, Waze becomes more valuable to its users. More value means more users, more data, and more value.

Yelp's reviews work similarly.

Yelp becomes more valuable when people or business owners add reviews and location information. Again, more people using Yelp leads to more data, which results in even more people using Yelp!

IMDB (the Internet Movie Database) leverages this network effect too.

Users add data about movies. The platform becomes more valuable. That value attracts more users. Those users add even more data.

Now think about this....

Would it be possible for another company to come along and do what IMDB does? Maybe.

Assuming that company has bottomless pockets and nearly endless amounts of time and resources. IMDB's database contains more than eight million titles. The website has 83 million registered users contributing data.

Nobody's going to compete because those numbers are so massive. Why bother pouring money into a similar venture when IMDB already has so much data that it can tank a rival before it even gets off the ground?

Data, in and of itself, isn't inherently valuable.

But if that data can be used to provide something users want and will contribute to themselves, you have data network effects in action.

Network Effect #6 – Being the Verb in a Category

If an American asks you for a tissue, they're not going to ask for a tissue. They'll ask for a Kleenex.

If they want something photocopied, they'll say they're going to Xerox it.

All video formats in the '80s and '90s boiled down to VHS. Later, DVD became the main format, followed by Blu-Ray, which demolished the concept of HD DVDs.

And there are plenty of examples from today we can also point to. People tell you to "Google it" when you need to find something online. When editing images, we say we'll, "Photoshop it."

It helps if your business name can become a verb. For example, if Xerox were called "ABC Quality Photocopiers," it wouldn't have become a verb.

These examples show the "being the verb in a category" network effect. This effect occurs when a product becomes so widely adopted that replacing it with anything similar is tough. The only way one of these products or services gets replaced is for something to come along that shakes things up so drastically that the entire industry changes!

THE CHICKEN OR THE EGG? GETTING STARTED WITH NETWORK EFFECTS

When we looked at Trulia's story, we saw the chicken and egg situation in action. It's the classic "What came first?" question.

You'll end up asking the same thing about your service with network effects. Only now, you're trying to figure out if the audience or service comes first. That's the problem Trulia had. There's no audience without listings. But who's going to provide listings when there's no audience?

The good news is that isn't an unanswerable question.

In Trulia's case, the listings came first because the platform could provide enough benefits to real estate agents willing to let Trulia index their listings. And you'll often find that one side of the equation is more complicated to solve than the other, which gives you your answer.

Uber is always looking for new drivers. It needs them so severely that sometimes it even pays drivers to join the platform. Those new drivers allow Uber to attract more customers, so the subsidization solves the chicken and egg problem in this example.

PayPal used to do something similar. You'd get $5 if you could get a new user to sign up. And another $5 went the new user's way to incentivize them. Of course, PayPal doesn't have to do that anymore because its network effects (and association with eBay) have led to it becoming an industry standard.

Sometimes, you may be able to leverage existing data to start filling out the supply side of your service. For example, let's say you're building a marketplace to link accountants with potential clients. You could pre-fill the accountants' listing pages using details pulled from their websites.

That will hopefully lead to some users visiting your platform.

You could then send those users to the accountants as leads, thus showcasing the platform's value. And now, you have ammunition to ask the accountants to sign up for a premium (and paid) subscription that results in even more leads.

This is almost precisely what urban.com.au did in the property development niche. It found out about new-build apartments and homes locally and created free listings for them. This attracted users to its platform. When a user inquired, urban.com.au sent it to the developer as a lead.

The developers loved getting those leads. So, they were more likely to start working with urban.com.au. In the end, the company managed to get developers to sign up for premium packages to get even more leads. It's an intelligent play.

ONE CLEVER STRATEGY A HAIRDRESSER MARKETPLACE USED TO GROW RAPIDLY

Another clever play is to build some software.

Styleseat did that in the hairdressing niche. Beyond being a marketplace for hairdressers and their clients, the platform also offers hairdressers software that helps them run their businesses. The software is free; Styleseat only asks for a credit card processing fee. In return, hairdressers get access to touch-free payments and helpful scheduling tools.

The value attracts the hairdressers.

The hairdressers attract the audience.

As the audience grows, even more hairdressers come on board.

Network effects win the day again.

My point is the chicken and egg situation is a quandary. But it's one you can solve with any number of approaches. Most of these involve focusing on the supply side of the equation. Offer suppliers some initial value to get them on board. Doing that gives you something to serve your audience, which will grow to the point where suppliers offer more.

The egg is hatched.

The chicken is born.

And you have a business on your hands!

PREVENTING PEOPLE FROM CIRCUMVENTING THE NETWORK

So, we've seen how practical network effects can be in helping build a robust subscription business. We've also noticed several types of network effects you can leverage.

Unfortunately, you'll face some challenges when trying to utilize this most important strategic factor. The biggest challenge?

Disintermediation.

That is a fancy word for a vulnerability that applies to most marketplace networks. It happens when a supplier and a customer connect through your platform. That's what you want to happen, of course. But that supplier and buyer then form a relationship and decide to leave the platform and just work together directly.

They cut out the middleman—you!

This is a problem in a subscription business. You want retention and repeat purchases to generate recurring revenue. If you can't retain your suppliers and consumers, everything falls apart.

There are many stories of seemingly booming businesses being forced to close their doors due to disintermediation. HomeJoy was a home cleaning startup that raised $40 million in funding before going under because too many of its users ended up cutting it out of the process.

TakeLessons, a San Diego-based company that links students with teachers, has battled this problem since its 2006 founding, despite being such a strong business that it raised $19 million in investor funding.

So...

How do you stop this from happening?

You can provide tools that network members can only access if they stick with you. Or you could rely on your business' reputation, and the desire suppliers may have to piggyback on that reputation to keep people on board. Some networks offer exclusive leads, as seen in the urban.com.au example.

How does this advice work in practice? Let's take Upwork as an example.

The dominant freelancing portal out there, Upwork links people who need jobs with expert freelancers who can do those jobs. Users get connected to people who can either supply or complete work.

Naturally, there's plenty of scope for disintermediation here. If a supplier uses a freelancer several times, they may suggest taking the relationship away from the platform.

Upwork fights this in several ways. For example, it offers payment protection facilities that ensure freelancers get paid for their work. This protects freelancers from doing a job only to get stiffed by somebody who never intended to pay.

You don't have those protections without the platform.

Upwork also has time tracking software that allows clients to confirm their freelancers are doing the work they're paying for. That's built into the platform and ensures suppliers aren't overpaying for the work they need.

Again, you don't get that protection without Upwork.

So, we see an example of a platform offering valuable tools that bring so much value that the desire to leave lowers. Does this mean disintermediation never happens with Upwork?

Of course not.

But these tools allow the platform to create a persuasive argument that taking a working relationship outside Upwork creates risk on both sides. Maybe that risk is high enough to dissuade many users from leaving the network.

Other ways to approach the problem depend on your type of business. Lyft and Uber get around the disintermediation problem by masking their drivers' phone numbers. A customer can't call a driver outside the platform if they don't have their number.

Tutor.com gradually reduces the percentage it claims from each transaction, starting at 50 percent and going down with each transaction.

And then some take the smart (albeit sneaky) approach.

Hired.com asks companies for $10,000 for its services. Naturally, many employers don't want to pay that. So, they attempt to disintermediate by contacting candidates outside of the platform. Hired.com overcame this by offering job seekers an incentive:

If they get a job, the platform sends them a $150 bottle of champagne.

Because of the champagne, most of the platform's job seekers were happy to let them know when they got a job. Hired.com would then ask for the hiring company's details for its records. If that company was a Hired.com customer, they got a new $10,000 invoice in the mail, even if they'd tried to circumvent the system that put them in touch with the candidate in the first place.

GAMIFICATION—BORROWING COMPUTER GAME CONCEPTS TO INCREASE ENGAGEMENT

I'd like to wrap up by touching on a concept that isn't a direct network effect—but is often leveraged by businesses and platforms with network effects.

Gamification involves offering incentives to keep people using a product. The term comes from video games, where players get "Achievements" or "Trophies" for doing certain things in their games. These rewards are often linked to activities that require the player to spend a lot of time in the game. For example, an online football game may give an achievement for scoring the most goals in online matches.

And people keep playing. For *hours*!

And the whole time, they're either paying a subscription to keep playing, or the game presents them with buyable bonus content.

So, gamification is used here to keep players engaged so developers can earn more over the long term.

In the world of subscription businesses, gamification becomes effective when a platform's community can see what other people are doing. The great minds at NFX call this "creating a multiplayer product."

With multiplayer products, users feel the presence of other users. For example, YouTube's comments and video view counters show the impact other users are having. Amazon does the same with reviews. Past product reviews help future buyers make purchasing decisions. Again, we see the effects of a multiplayer environment.

Returning to the gaming world's achievements systems, both Xbox and PlayStation allow players to see what others have achieved. If you have a friend who owns the same game, it's easy to check their achievements. If they have something you don't, that could incentivize you to keep playing the game, thus deepening your engagement. That happens because of the multiplayer environment these platforms cultivate.

Engagement is what you're shooting for with gamification.

Deeper engagement means more time spent using a platform. More time on the platform leads to more chances for profit as "players" interact with one another—in addition to the gamified elements of the platform. Ultimately, deeper engagement strengthens network effects, which is only good for your business.

GAMIFYING YOUR PRODUCT—SOME QUICK TIPS

If gamification sounds like an excellent way to create engagement for your platform, you'll need some tips on implementing it into your subscription business. I won't go too in-depth here. Instead, here are a couple of quick tips that will help you gamify quickly so you can start building engagement.

Tip 1 – Figure Out How to Reward Users at Each Stage of Their Journey

Your users want to feel like they're rewarded for making progress. So, find a way to give them a little dopamine rush for doing something you want them to do inside your platform.

The language app Duolingo does a great job of this. It grants users "Gold" status whenever they complete a lesson. For further engagement, this "Gold" status decays when the lesson is not revisited. It's restored when the user goes back and completes the lesson again.

By doing this, Duolingo offers a reward for lesson completion and an incentive to revisit and repeat the lesson—which is vital because repetition is one of the keys to learning a new language.

Tip 2 – Integrate a Social Element

When I mentioned the multiplayer element of gamification earlier, I was talking about the social aspect. If you can find ways to connect your platform's users, you give them a reason to keep coming back.

There are many ways to do this.

Simple scoreboards may be a good idea if your product has challenges you use to rank people. Users may return to beat their old score and get ahead of people above them on the leaderboard. We did this in our Archistar Academy product. Every time you viewed a course or completed an exam, you would get more points awarded for more challenging courses. Tons of students competed to be ranked #1 in the world!

You can also offer your users the ability to form communities within your platform. These communities create friendship, which is difficult to give up once established. Mobile apps, such as Clash of Clans, do this well.

Then, there's the option of allowing people to share their achievements with others. Fitness apps like MyFitnessPal use this technique. Users can share their runs and personal records on social media, which prompts conversation and gets more people involved. And if that sharing brings more people to sign up to your platform, then congratulations—you have network effects in action!

LEVERAGE THE POWER OF NETWORK EFFECTS

I'll repeat it...

I believe network effects are the most powerful of the strategic subscription factors. Hopefully, the examples I've provided in this chapter make that clear. And with some luck, you may now know how to leverage network effects for your own business.

If your product or service becomes more valuable as usage increases, you are highly defensible. While the other strategic factors help you deepen and widen your moat, network effects let you create an impenetrable fortress that competitors will smash up against if they somehow manage to make it past the moat.

Focus on this strategic factor. Figure out how you can leverage network effects in your business. Once you've done that, you can move on to the next chapter, where we'll focus on how you can boost revenue without hiring a massive sales team.

> **ACTION EXERCISE: HOW CAN YOU LEVERAGE NETWORK EFFECTS IN YOUR BUSINESS?**

_____

_____

_____

_____

_____

CHAPTER SEVEN

LAND AND EXPAND: LIFTING REVENUE WITHOUT HIRING A HUGE SALES TEAM

It was May 2013, and Jack Conte was utterly exhausted.

But it was a good kind of exhaustion. Jack had spent most of the past fifty days building an elaborate replica of the Millennium Falcon from *Star Wars*. Long eighteen-hour days had finally resulted in a set he could use to shoot his latest music video.

He was tired.

But he was also thrilled about the prospect of his audience seeing what he'd come up with.

Once the music video was in the can, he uploaded it to his YouTube channel. One hundred thousand subscribers lapped it up, along with many more people who weren't subscribers.

But Jack had a problem—he'd maxed out every credit card he had to make his music video a reality.

But he also had a potential solution.

Along with his friend, Sam, he'd created a new platform called Patreon. Through the platform, anybody who enjoyed Jack's work would be able to make donations to his next project or simply pay him for his work on his *Star Wars* video.

Jack popped the link to his newly created platform into his video's description. Within a couple of weeks, that platform had wholly changed the economics of Jack's YouTube channel. Instead of relying on his new video's $100 or so in ad revenue, he received $5,000 in funding from "Patreons," who wanted to see more of what he did.

A good idea was buried in Jack's new platform.

HOW PATREON STUMBLED UPON THE PERFECT GROWTH ENGINE

With Patreon, Jack could provide creators with a way to get paid for their work directly from the people who consumed the content. Through this platform, creators would no longer be tied down to the terms (and lackluster ad revenue-sharing models) of the platforms they used to host their content.

Jack's success created a buzz that quickly attracted funding and users to his budding platform. Soon, creators signed up in droves to use Patreon to deliver content and get paid fairly. They started using the platform to set up their own mini-subscription businesses, with followers committing to paying monthly to receive exclusive content. Other people could pay one-off fees to receive specific content—meaning Patreon offered various ways creators could get paid.

A new business had landed. Now, it needed to expand.

I won't go into the details of how Patreon achieved its first round of seed funding or how the business has grown since the early days of 2013. Instead, I want to focus on what Patreon is doing with its pricing and how it has used the land and expand strategy to grow.

Patreon has two pricing models.

The first is usage-based.

It charges a flat percentage of creators' earnings, allowing the creator to pay based on how much they use the platform. You may remember this as the usage-based pricing system we've already discussed.

This is a perfect land and expand strategy.

Creators only pay based on what they earn. New creators don't have to pay through the nose for Patreon's services. Instead, the platform allows for minimal payments (landing the client in the process) and then expands based on the client's success. If the content creator blows up and starts earning a lot more money, Patreon makes more too.

That second part is the "expand" aspect of the strategy.

But eventually, Patreon will run into a problem with this pricing model. The more successful creators may resent giving so much of their earnings to the platform, leading them to look into other options.

Patreon's solution?

Their second pricing model: a subscription!

Patreon created a sister site called Memberful, which allows content creators to sign up and access many of the same benefits that Patreon offers. The difference is that Memberful members pay a monthly subscription and a lower transaction percentage.

So, we see a combination of pricing methods. Plus, we see a brilliant land and expand strategy that pulls creators in, grows with them, and then moves them to a recurring subscription model once they get big enough.

And Patreon did it all without having to build a massive sales team.

Therein lies the critical benefit of the land and expand strategy. Instead of asking a client to sign up for a large contract (or an expensive subscription) upfront, you let them try your platform before committing to it. That may be through a free trial, a small order, a single software license, or, as in Patreon's case, a usage-based model that results in the client only getting charged based on how much they use (or earn from) the service.

The great thing about land and expand is that it brings more people to your product.

If those people like what you're doing, they will tell others about it. That means subscription value grows over time (expand!) because you're landing more clients with the help of your existing ones.

It's network effects. It's a referral. And it's providing value to clients while allowing them to see what's so awesome about your platform.

Best of all...it's something any small business can do!

HOW A LOCAL BAKERY "LANDS AND EXPANDS" INTO CAFÉS AND RESTAURANTS

My local bakery is a great example. It uses this strategy to get its products into as many local cafés as possible. The bakery gives free samples of every type of bread it makes to the cafés and lets them know they have no minimum order quantity. The cafés try the free samples, love them, and order the amount they're comfortable with. Over time, those orders grow in size as the bakery's products become more entrenched in the café's menu.

Land and expand.

In this chapter, we'll dig into the meat of this strategy so you can leverage it for your own business.

EXPLAINING THE LAND AND EXPAND STRATEGY

The idea behind land and expand is to build consumer confidence in a new product or service.

You want to get people to take a chance on you, which they're unlikely to do if you ask for a hefty subscription fee upfront for something they've never used (and perhaps don't even understand).

Again, Patreon had that problem.

Before Patreon, content creators relied on the platforms they used to pay them. For YouTube creators like Jack Conte, that meant hoping to make enough ad revenue to justify making videos.

Patreon offered a new way to get paid, which relied on the goodwill of subscribers and fans.

It was a novel concept.

It was also one that many creators felt wouldn't work, as evidenced by the fact that none of the forty creators Jack told the idea to in the early days signed up. Only after Jack achieved personal success with Patreon did people become interested. To maintain that interest, Jack made it possible for creators to join and start making money.

So, the "I don't understand this new product" problem disappeared.

That's what land and expand will also do for your business.

By starting small and making it easy for people to experience what you're offering, you're giving them a chance to learn about the product. That learning experience isn't the most profitable for you, at least in the short term. But it showcases what your product can do, which means you attract new clients.

Once you've landed the client, you start expanding. Patreon claims more money as the content creator grows. The bakery I mentioned lands bigger deals with the cafés it supplies. Your subscription business may be able to guide the client toward a subscription that gives them even more benefits in return for a recurring fee.

It's a simple concept.

Start small. Land clients. Expand what you offer (and what you receive) from those clients. Grow your business.

But don't let this simplicity fool you—there are ways to mess up the land and expand strategy. And the biggest one is to assume the plan's only goal is to attract as many people as possible.

That's a big part of it, but not the only factor!

Land and expand is about the relationships you form with clients you attract to your service. Again, we can take my little local bakery as an example. It's not just shipping out free samples and hoping cafés will order from it. It's building relationships with café owners by offering a quality product and showing them how they can get more of it.

Communication is vital when it comes to land and expand.

It's not just about your users getting access to the product. It's about helping them see how fantastic that product is so you can guide them toward expanding their usage (and thus expanding how much they're paying you).

Ultimately, land and expand enables product-led growth.

Users can find the product and sign up to use it—in whatever small landing form that product takes—without needing you to push them. Assuming the product somehow delivers what it promises and benefits the user, they'll be willing to pay for an expanded version.

Along the way, you're forced to make your product better. If you're landing clients only to see them drop off before expanding, that tells you there's a problem. Something isn't working as it should, so people aren't staying engaged.

So, the land and expand strategy allows you to iteratively improve your product or service, often with the help of user feedback, in ways a traditional sales strategy can't.

THE FIVE FACTORS NEEDED TO SUCCESSFULLY EXECUTE LAND AND EXPAND

So, you know what land and expand is—and you've seen that it can work for all sorts of businesses. Now, you need to know how to implement the strategy to help you grow your business.

To do that, we need to understand the key factors that underpin a successful land and expand:

Factor #1 – An Attractive Initial Offer

Land and expand is not about trying to sell large upfront deals. If you're thinking of hiring a sales team and pelting the market with offers to sign up for your expensive subscription right off the bat, you're doing the opposite of land and expand.

With land and expand, you need to offer users the chance to try before they buy. That means coming up with an offer that draws people in and helps them overcome any hesitation they may have about using a new product or service.

I've highlighted ways you can do this already—free trials, usage-based pricing, and having no minimum order restrictions all work here. The crucial part is that you don't give these new users *everything*.

Offer your minimum viable product to show them the offering works for them. Or maybe the whole product, but for a limited time or a limited number of users.

Once you've landed them, you start pushing toward expansion. In a subscription business, that means gently guiding users toward a recurring subscription payment.

Factor #2 – A Product-Market Fit

An easy way for people to land on your product means nothing if the product doesn't fit the market. If people don't need it, they will not use it. And that won't change just because you're giving it away for free.

Let's look at Patreon again.

That product has a significant market fit. Why?

Content creators often feel like they don't get paid enough for the work they put in. That's especially the case on YouTube, where a video that gets 100,000 views only generates as little as $100 (at least in Jack Conte's case).

Creators want more ways to get paid. They want as many income streams as possible, and, much like you, they want recurring and reliable revenue. Patreon offers all that, which is why it's a fantastic product that fits its market.

Your product needs to have a similar fit. And you'll know you've gotten this right if you're seeing high growth, high retention, and a solid net promoter score.

Factor #3 – Re-Earning the Business

Let's look at using land and expand with a subscription model. You've officially landed a user if you can get them to subscribe to your service.

Great work! Now...how are you going to keep them subscribed?

For some businesses, this is relatively easy. If you're offering an ongoing service that integrates into whatever the user does, they'll see the continued value and stay subscribed.

However, if what you're offering has a shelf life, you need to come up with ways to create value beyond what attracted the user to your platform in the first place. You need to re-earn their business to keep them subscribed. That means constantly looking for ways to create value so your users aren't tempted to seek another service that offers something better than yours.

Mailchimp is a good example. It lets users send marketing emails for free for up to 2,000 users. And as you grow, you'll be charged. It also has other relevant marketing tools that small business owners want to use, like a website builder and postcard sender.

This is a crucial part of your expansion, and it's why you want to hold back on offering everything in free or early subscription tiers.

Factor #4 – Solid Onboarding

Do you remember the main problem land and expand is supposed to help you overcome?

I'll give you a second....

Lack of familiarity!

If a potential user isn't familiar with your product or service, they will not pay a premium price for it. They want to try before they buy, which is why you have free tiers and small offers to land them.

But the small offer isn't enough to overcome that lack of familiarity. You still need to teach users how to use your platform, especially if introducing a new idea to the industry.

That means one of two things:

1. Being so easy to use that you don't need any onboarding; or
2. Providing solid onboarding to help users understand how to use the features you're making available.

Onboarding can take the form of video walkthroughs, guided tutorials, or any other tool you can think of to help new users get to grips with your platform. Sometimes you even need a customer success representative to offer one-on-one onboarding. And suppose you can include information in your onboarding about how the expanded version of the platform will help the user do even more. In that case, you're on your way to building a profitable relationship with your user.

Factor #5 – A Funnel

If you're not using a huge sales team to pull off the land and expand strategy, what are you using?

A sales funnel that has a healthy heaping of network effects thrown in.

In other words, you want to ensure your platform's users have everything they need to engage with the platform, with each other, and with the types of people you want to attract.

Here are a few things that can help with that:

- Incorporate sharing buttons into your marketing content and anything that's sharable within your platform. For example, users of MyFitnessPal have the option to share their workout stats on social media. Those shares

- get more eyes on the product, leading to more users landing on it.
- Encourage existing users to write reviews and post on social media what they're getting from the platform. A lot of them won't do it. But some will. And of those, many will have friends and associates who also need what your platform offers.
- Create content that talks about the platform and its benefits. If you can share user success stories, you'll have valuable social proof that goes a long way toward convincing other people to give your platform a try.

Those are just a few quick ideas.

The key here is to figure out ways to get the people who are using your product or service to start talking about it. By doing that, you turn those users into a sales team that will help you land more clients.

HOW DO YOU KNOW IF LAND AND EXPAND IS WORKING?

You're landing clients, and your platform is growing. At least the number of people using it is developing, which is a good sign. But is that enough to show you that your land and expand strategy is working?

Not necessarily.

Increasing the number of customers you're landing only matters if you get the expand part right. You end up with many customers and no profit if you're not. Think back to Ethan Stock's story in Chapter Six. A growing business that makes no money isn't a business. So, it's clear that you need to track metrics beyond the number of customers you have to confirm that land and expand is working for you.

What are those metrics? I have some lists for you.

The Revenue Metrics

When it comes to revenue, these are the metrics to keep an eye on:

- Monthly Recurring Revenue – You're building a subscription business. Achieving recurring revenue is a crucial component. This metric tells you if you're getting recurring revenue, thus creating the predictability you're looking for.
- Annual Contract Value – How much money are you making, on average, per customer annually? More importantly, is that number growing thanks to the expansion you've put in place?
- Revenue Growth Rate – If your total revenue shows consistent growth, that's usually a good indicator that you're landing people and (crucially) that a good portion of them are expanding.

User Metrics

Are your users getting what they need out of your platform to the point where they want to expand their usage? These metrics will help you figure out the answer:

- Customer Lifetime Value (LTV) – How much money does the average customer spend with you over the lifetime of their use of your platform? This is a metric you hopefully won't be able to figure out for a few years at least. After all, the whole point of a subscription is to keep people paying a recurring fee for as long as possible. Once you know your LTV, you can determine if you're spending too much to land your customers.
- Annual Renewal Rate – Ideally, you want this to be as high as possible. Any low numbers here, and, likely, subscribers aren't getting what they need from your platform.
- Customer Acquisition Costs (CAC) – What are your sales and marketing costs to acquire a new customer? Tie this one into your customer lifetime value metric. You want CAC to be a third or less of LTV.

Some Additional Metrics

Beyond those highlighted above, there are other, less tangible metrics you may want to keep an eye on.

"Stickiness" is a big one. Are the users who landed on your platform exploring its features? Are they utilizing those features and showing interest in the extra stuff they could get if they paid a little more? You have a sticky product if you can say "yes" to both questions.

That's a good thing for any subscription business.

MAKING LAND AND EXPAND WORK—DOCUSIGN'S KEYS TO SUCCESS

I've spent most of this chapter sharing practical advice and information about what land and expand is and how you can make it work. How about we now zero in on a company that used this strategy to grow to tremendous heights?

DocuSign was founded in 2003 with a simple idea: to provide an e-signature solution that allows users to send, receive, and sign digital documents. The key to success for this model is its multi-tier subscription approach.

Naturally, the lowest tier offered the most basic functionality. There were (and still are) limitations on the number of documents a user could send out for a signature. The platform only offers access to a single user at the lowest level and only allows for creating documents that collect basic information.

Still, users get access to templates. Plus, they can integrate the platform with the likes of Google Drive and Dropbox. There's enough to make the platform attractive without needing a concerted sales push.

What you're seeing with this lowest tier is a brilliant land and expand strategy in action. Individual users get to see what's possible with DocuSign for a small monthly fee. If they like what they see, they can expand into one of the company's high-tier subscriptions, such as Business Pro, which allows for multiple users and unlimited documents.

The strategy worked. DocuSign is the industry standard and has become "the verb" in the e-signature sector. In the first quarter of 2021, the company achieved a 54 percent growth rate. It also boasts a 125 percent net dollar retention rate.

Simply put, DocuSign made land and expand work.

So...how did they do it?

DocuSign has done several crucial things that allowed land and expand to work. These are the keys to DocuSign's success, which you may be able to adapt to your own business.

Key #1 – Establishing Key Strengths and then Scaling

I touched on the idea of offering a minimum viable product to land clients a little earlier in the chapter. That's precisely what DocuSign did by focusing on its e-signature solution. The company now offers a lot more than that. But it still focuses on this key strength of its service to land new clients.

Once it's landed new clients, DocuSign builds on its key strength to scale up by offering additional services beyond the e-signatures. Sometimes, that just means allowing users to send and receive *more* documents. But in its highest tiers, DocuSign offers functionality for branding, collecting payments, bulk sending, and other helpful stuff that builds on the base service.

So, it lands with the simple key strength of e-signatures. Then, it expands into the related stuff that people who use this service may also be interested in.

It's working out pretty well for the company's margins too. In 2019, DocuSign had an operating margin of 11 percent. In the first quarter of 2021, that had grown to 29 percent. Establishing a strength, using it as a minimum viable product to land customers, and then expanding on that strength has been a vital part of this growth.

Key #2 – Creating a New Industry Standard for Trust

Like many companies that use the land and expand strategy, DocuSign overcame the unfamiliarity hurdle in 2003. The concept of e-signatures was new, and no industry standards existed for how to do them.

So, DocuSign created those standards.

The company formed a Board of Governors to serve as the driving force of its proprietary xDTM standard. It even had a snazzy analogy to lean on:

"What the PCI Standard is to Payments, the xDTM Standard is to Digital Transactions."

This clever move also involved setting up eight areas of trust that users could judge the new standard on.

With its xDTM standard, DocuSign found a way to differentiate itself using one of the more complex aspects of its business. And in doing so, it managed to demonstrate the security of e-signatures in a way its competitors couldn't, setting a new industry standard and building trust, which led to more landing (and expanding).

Key #3 – Leveraging Equity Financing Strategically

Equity investment played a crucial role in DocuSign's ability to expand.

The company created extensive partnerships with companies like Google, SAP, Microsoft, Intel, Dell, Salesforce, and FedEx. You might recognize all of those brands. More importantly, you might recognize them all as brands that might facilitate (or use) something like e-signatures.

The partnerships were perfect!

DocuSign received equity investment and built connections with companies that put it in a position to tap into new markets. Again, no sales team was required. By leveraging its partners' brands and scale, DocuSign entered new markets while making its business more defensible.

After all, competitors will struggle to do business with these companies if DocuSign already has working agreements with them!

Key #4 – The Continued Potential for International Growth

Sticking with the expand side of things, DocuSign always had the potential to grow far beyond its initial offering of an e-signature service. We see this in the array of extra services it now offers at the higher tiers of its subscription model.

But that's not the only expansion potential it has.

As I write this, DocuSign only generates 21 percent of its total revenue outside the United States. That's something the company is very aware of.

It's already carrying out that expansion.

DocuSign's international sales grew by 84 percent between the first quarter of 2021 and the first quarter of 2022. In January 2020, the company's Head of Enterprise Solutions, Eduardo Martinez, even wrote an extensive blog post about the "European SaaS opportunity" and how DocuSign wanted to be a big part of it.

This is not a company that is happy to land in the US and stay there.

DocuSign has a significant opportunity to expand internationally—barring language changes; there's not a vast amount it needs to modify in its platform to do it successfully.

So, the key here... Room for scale!

Key #5 – Category Creation and Expansion

One of the most critical aspects of building a subscription business is finding ways to guard against, and separate yourself from, your competition.

DocuSign did that with its bold category creation strategy.

The company essentially created the field of Digital Transaction Management, highlighting it as the key to digital transformation.

Once this was established, it expanded into a new category—System of Agreement.

The second category offers DocuSign's services as an enterprise-scale solution. With System of Agreement, users can integrate a ton of back- and front-end stakeholders into the agreements they sign with DocuSign and automate a lot of their work.

These bold moves furthered the company's expansion. They also solidified DocuSign as the industry standard for the entire sector, meaning even more users would land with them.

Key #6 – The DocuSign Global Trust Network

In 2013, DocuSign introduced its Global Trust Network to provide a best-in-class amalgamation of all of its most essential services. The network's purpose is right in its name—building trust. The network offers proprietary security services (that the company developed itself) to ensure those who signed up get their documents authenticated in the most appropriate ways for their transactions.

It was (and still is) a huge success.

In 2015, DocuSign raised $233 million in investor funding for its Global Trust Network. The following year, the company announced that the network had experienced 125 percent year-on-year growth. And as of 2018, the network had signed up more than 450,000 companies across 188 countries, giving it 400 million users.

If you want an example of expansion, this is it!

The Global Trust Network was introduced a decade after DocuSign burst onto the scene with its e-signature service. And its introduction brings us right back to the first key in the company's success story:

Land with something that showcases your strength.

Expand on that strength with something that your market needs. In this case, added security in the era of cloud computing was a market need. The Global Trust Network was the perfect fit.

PREPARE FOR LANDING

Start small by focusing on landing customers using free trials and small offers so you can get them onto your platform. Once they're entrenched and finding value, expand by offering additional services they'll find helpful.

Begin by focusing on your platform's core strengths, just as DocuSign did with its e-signature service. Once the market recognizes your platform as the go-to for your most important service, focus on expanding beyond that service by building upon it with related products.

Land with something small. Expand into something unique.

It's a strategy that has reinforced many a subscription business. And by following it, you can build a foundation of users that allows for scaling in the future.

ACTION EXERCISE:

How can you implement land and expand in your business?

_____

_____

_____

_____

_____

CHAPTER EIGHT

QUICK WAYS TO GROW CLIENT NUMBERS ON A SHOESTRING BUDGET

We're deep into the book now, and I know you have something important on your mind...

Client numbers.

Specifically, how do you grow client numbers when you don't have millions of dollars to spend on marketing? After all, a subscription business isn't much use if you don't have clients. The people who subscribe to your product or service are the lifeblood of your venture. Without them, you just have something that costs you money to maintain.

So, how do you get clients?

And more importantly...how do you get them on a shoestring budget?

That's the question we'll answer in this chapter as we look at some techniques you can use, along with examples of companies that have leveraged them to bulk up their numbers.

THE FOUR TECHNIQUES YOU CAN USE TO GROW MEMBERSHIP NUMBERS

I will start this section with a bit of a cheap plug....

If you pick up my book *Feed a Starving Crowd*, you'll find 227 strategies you can use to grow your membership numbers. If you're serious about doing everything possible to get your numbers up, grab a copy and do everything in it that applies to your business.

But let's say you want a quick start.

My previous book can wait—you want some techniques you can start implementing today.

That's what we're going to look at here.

The four essential techniques I will share with you are my go-to methods for growing client numbers. Some of them are 100 percent free to use. Others require a small investment, though not so much that you'll break the bank.

And all of them are effective.

Let's jump in with...

TECHNIQUE #1 – LEVERAGE COMMUNITY MARKETING

Community marketing has been a go-to technique for SaaS businesses for years.

Take LiveAgent, which offers help desk software, as an example. Former Head of Marketing Matej Kukucka points out how the company uses the power of community to get its message out there:

"We run our community on Facebook because it's where most of the SaaS communities are being hosted. We have been running our community for more than a year now.

"Our community is the best way to inform customers about upcoming updates and new features."

He talks about how staying in constant touch with LiveAgent's community improves customer satisfaction. And while this doesn't always lead directly to sales, it does accomplish two things:

1. It keeps existing customers happy so they continue using the service.
2. It gives existing customers an excellent service they're likely to talk about with others who need it.

The second one is where the community element comes in.

You build a community around your product by staying in touch with the people you already have. That community can then evangelize on your behalf and bring more people into the fold.

Let's look at another example....

Airbase offers spending management software. According to its Event Marketing Manager, Laura Grandi-Hill, Slack is the company's tool of choice for building a community:

"Our community, Off the Ledger, runs on Slack. It has been running since November of 2019 and now has a membership of over 1,500!

"It's a finance and accounting community that helps Airbase grow by giving us a steady pipeline of guest bloggers and webinar speakers (which has included finance leaders from SeatGeek, Uber, and more)."

I love this one.

First, thanks to the Slack community, you have membership within a membership.

That community empowers Airbase to use webinars (we'll get to those in just a moment) to share information and build client numbers. Laura also says prospects who join this community are more likely to convert into paying members than those who don't join.

Building a community around your business means having people who love what you're offering ready to go to bat for you.

Best of all, most of the tools you might use to build this community are either free or cheap. It doesn't cost a penny to set up a Facebook group. And you're not breaking the bank to set up a

Slack group, especially when it generates a positive ROI from new members and enhanced marketing opportunities.

Keep your community happy, and you can leverage it to grow that very same community.

TECHNIQUE #2 – USE WEBINARS TO ATTRACT NEW MEMBERS (AND RETAIN EXISTING ONES)

I said we'd be getting back to webinars!

A while back, I ran a product launch webinar for Dr. Libby Weaver (a well-known nutritional biochemist) that attracted almost 8,000 attendees. We came within a hair's breadth of breaking the world record at the time. And that webinar resulted in signing up many clients.

Why?

Webinars give you a chance to put a face (and a voice) to your product or service. They allow you to speak to your potential clients without asking them to spend time or money traveling to a seminar.

Watching a webinar is something that your prospective clients can do from their homes. That makes the clients easy to engage with, meaning you can hit more significant attendance numbers.

But that's not the only advantage of webinars. As a business owner, you don't have to spend much money to run one. You just need a decent microphone and some slides (camera optional!).

And once you have the first two, you can use them to record as many webinars as you want. Those webinars don't have to be "one-and-done" events.

Record them. Use them as lead magnets. Allow your webinars to keep pulling people in long after you've held the event!

You can use webinars to show people what your product or service looks like in action. You can share success stories, answer questions, and start tackling all of the obstacles that might prevent somebody from signing up for your subscription business.

At Archistar, we host a webinar once a month or so. Webinars are still one of our top acquisition methods for signing up new subscribers.

How do you structure a webinar?

Many options exist, but the best webinar is one where you feel comfortable. I used to use a precise format and plan every single element perfectly. With more experience now, I'm far more relaxed on the exact structure and recommend generally covering the following topics:

- An introduction to you and your background. Bonus points if you have a guest host who introduces you. (It's always better for others to say nice things about you than bragging about yourself.)
- Interesting content not readily available online. I love a good product pitch, and, from experience, attendees are also okay with being pitched, as long as they've learned something new first!

- Social proof involving people who have used your product or service talking about how awesome it is.
- A call to action that prompts people to sign up for your subscription or something else that moves them further down your sales funnel—maybe a personalized demo with the sales team.
- A Q&A section that allows you to overcome some common objections.

The Q&A section is underrated and often forgotten. In my webinars, it sometimes goes for up to an hour past the scheduled finish time, and the majority of attendees still hang around to hear more. The Q&A section is also an excellent opportunity to "get out in the open" concerns people may have but don't verbalize.

And with the call to action, I usually offer a "fast mover discount" if they can sign up within the next hour. I only provide a discount if there's a valid reason, and the fast-mover deal is reasonable because it saves our sales team from needing to follow up and run a personalized demo. So, I'm happy to pass those savings on to the subscriber. I share that with the audience for total transparency, which is always well received.

TECHNIQUE #3 – CREATE A CUSTOMER REFERRAL PROGRAM

Why have a referral program?

I'm about to hit you with some stats that will redefine that question. Instead of asking why you should have a referral program, ask yourself how you could *not* have one!

According to the report *What You Should Know About B2B Referrals—But Probably Don't*, published by advocate marketing firm Influitive, 69 percent of B2B professionals say that referral leads close faster than *any other type of lead*.

The same report shows that 71 percent of people say referral programs have the highest conversion rate of any marketing strategy.

Still not convinced?

Jack Morton Worldwide published a report in 2012 that taught us that 49 percent of people hear about brands first from their friends or family. That number is sure to be much higher in the age of social media. The message here is simple: people tell others about the brands they enjoy interacting with. So, referral programs increase brand awareness.

Need more?

Nielsen points out that 84 percent of people trust word of mouth from friends and family more than any marketing messages you put out.

Wharton shows us that a referred customer has a lifetime value 16 percent higher than a non-referred customer. Deloitte tells us that referred customers have a 37 percent higher retention rate than other customers.

And to top it all off, churn in referral channels is 18 percent lower than for any other channel.

Simply put, referrals work when it comes to growing client numbers and keeping numbers up.

And much like the other techniques on this list, setting up a referral program doesn't cost much money. You just need to figure out a way to offer your existing customers something that makes referring others worth their time.

That "something" could be a discount on your subscription. Maybe the referrer and the referred customer each gets a free month. Or your referrers could get access to exclusive content or services they wouldn't get if they didn't refer anybody.

The sky's the limit in terms of what you can offer. And by making those offers, you start pulling in more clients for your business while keeping your existing client base happy.

The result: You keep the foundation of clients you have now while constantly building up.

There's just one caveat to this technique....

If you use a referral program, you must ensure your service is everything you promise. If you start breaking customer promises, you'll find your customers disappear faster than you can shake a stick.

Getting referrals is one of my favorite techniques for bumping up client numbers. So, I think it's worth going into a lot more detail on this one. I'm going to share some of the referral strategies you could use to hit the types of numbers I just talked about.

Strategy #1 - One-Time Cashback

Sometimes you have to spend a little to get a lot.

In other words, a little cash incentive now can lead to referrals that make a lot of money for your business in the future. By offering one-time cashback for a referral, you get a guaranteed client worth much more than the amount you spent on the gift.

How does this work? Payroll and HR systems provider Gusto offers a perfect example.

It has a "Refer and Earn" program.

Existing clients get a referral link they can share on social media, email, or even their own website. Potential clients click the link, sign up for Gusto, and get a free trial. In return, the referrer receives a cash gift card they can spend however they'd like.

But here's the critical component.... That gift card only goes out if the referred client *signs up to Gusto.*

The gift is triggered when the company receives the first invoice payment from the referred customer. If there's no invoice, there's no cash gift. And if there's no cash gift, Gusto hasn't paid a dollar for the exposure they just got.

If the referred person does sign up, Gusto doesn't lose out either.

Why? The first invoice will always be more than the amount they give to the referrer as a gift. It's all so simple.

Offer a little cash to your existing customers to get new people to sign up. Ensure you collect money from the new customer before paying the referrer.

BOOM!

You have a new client and a happy existing client who just got a nice little reward for doing something as simple as posting a referral link.

Strategy #2 - Unlock Features or Upgrades

We're going to revisit our friends at Dropbox for this example.

Dropbox goes the route of offering users more storage space for referrals. If you have a Dropbox Basic account, you get an extra 500MB of storage for every person you refer, up to a maximum of 16 GB.

So, you can refer up to thirty-two people.

With Dropbox Plus or Dropbox Professional, you get 1 GB of additional storage per referral up to a maximum of 32 GB.

Again, thirty-two people.

I love two things about this referral program.

First, offering new features or upgrades means giving your existing customers more of what they came for. In Dropbox's case, more storage is something any customer wants.

The second is the limitation. By capping referrals at thirty-two people, Dropbox ensures it is getting high-quality referrals. It also means existing customers can't get so much storage that there's no chance they'll ever need to pay Dropbox to get more.

So, this type of referral is simple:

Offer something extraordinary that holds value to your users. Don't offer so much that you shoot yourself in the foot to get a new client.

Strategy #3 - A Free Month of Subscription

I touched on this one earlier when talking about the "something" you could offer as part of a referral program. A free month's subscription is worth its weight in gold to your users. At least, it should be as long as you've built a proper business offering.

Evernote is an excellent example of how to use this strategy.

It gives out points for successful referrals. When the existing customer has gathered enough points, they can trade them in for either a free month or a *free year* of Evernote Personal.

Here's the rub....

To get enough points for a free subscription period, the existing customer has to refer enough people that they essentially pay for that free period through other people's subscriptions.

Evernote isn't losing out here. It is building its client base while rewarding loyal customers, which is basically what you aim to do with any referral strategy.

The use of points is a nice touch too.

That gives Evernote complete control over how much work a referrer has to do to earn enough points to get their free month. It also lays the groundwork for a loyalty program offering more rewards.

There'll be a lot more on loyalty programs later.

Strategy #4 - Branded Swag

This one is simple.

If your company has an attractive logo or brand, you can send branded swag to your referrers. T-shirts, mugs, pens—anything else that's even slightly useful—can have your brand slapped on it and be sent out to your most loyal referrers.

There's just one caveat to this strategy.... You need to have a brand people want on their stuff.

For example, Harley Davidson's customers will love swag with the Harley on it because they've bought into the brand already. But if you're running a SaaS accounting software model, you might find that your clients aren't too excited about wearing T-shirts with your logo plastered on them. Although at Archistar, branded T-shirts and caps are *very* popular with our client base; we see them worn everywhere!

Roses Only, a popular online florist in Australia, famously sold high-quality branded umbrellas below cost. On a rainy day in Sydney, thousands of people would advertise their brand—clever play!

Branded swag works best if you have a brand people recognize or are happy to be seen wearing or using.

Strategy #5 - Ongoing Referral Fees

Instead of offering a one-time cash incentive, you can provide ongoing rewards to your referrers.

I have personal experience with this one (as a referrer), thanks to Ontraport.

Ontraport is a sales and marketing platform I used in the early 2010s. I used it so much that my marketing agency ended up signing on as an affiliate with the brand.

Why? For every person we referred to sign up, we'd receive 30 percent of the revenue Ontraport earned from that person....

And we'd get that 30 percent *for the lifetime of the referred person's account.*

So, Ontraport essentially became a passive revenue stream for the business. I just needed to work to find people to refer to the company. Ontraport still has a similar program, though it now pays 25 percent instead of 30 percent. It's a program that will always encourage people to refer.

But again, there's a caveat.

Offering a chunk of revenue from a referred customer's account will affect your profit margins. You must ensure your margins are high enough to eat that expense while still making money from that customer. Otherwise, you're just growing a client base while your profits stagnate.

I believe this issue is responsible for Ontraport dropping its rate from 30 percent to 25 percent. That extra 5 percent in the Ontraport kitty ensures this strategy remains viable for the company. And as long as you can strike the right balance between reward and profit margin, it's a great way to grow client numbers while keeping existing clients happy.

Strategy #6 – Associated Businesses

A long time ago, I ran a marketing workshop for a group of local dance studio owners. We ran through an exercise where I asked them to do something simple:

Make a list of every business they could think of associated with their company.

They devised an extensive list of ideas—art schools, preschools, and swim schools all had students interested in learning new things. There were some local companies selling dance shoes and apparel. The studio owners came up with various businesses that were related to them somehow.

With that list ready, I asked them to do something else:

Get in touch with each of those businesses to suggest a partnership.

The studio would refer its clients to every business that said yes in return for the associated companies doing the same for the dance studio. The studio had a referral network in no time, with each business supporting the other. And the thing cost *nothing* to set up.

The lesson?

Mutually beneficial relationships between businesses can lead to massive increases in client numbers. So, I want you to run through the same exercise I had the dance studio owners do.

Make your list of associated businesses. Then, pick up the phone and start calling people (or email or connect on LinkedIn if more appropriate). Every business that comes on board is a potential source of new clients for your company.

TECHNIQUE #4 – USE EMBEDDED INTEGRATION TO MAKE YOUR SERVICE INDISPENSABLE

We've already talked about the workplace messaging app Slack. This company has a fantastic value proposition that pulls in customers. But as I said earlier, the value prop alone isn't enough to keep Slack at the top of the heap.

So, how does Slack maintain its position while acquiring new clients?

I could go on for days answering that question. But one of its most essential techniques involves making itself indispensable to the businesses that use it.

How? Integrating with almost every app or piece of software you can think of.

Currently, Slack integrates with more than 2,000 apps. These include major players like OneDrive, DocuSign, Google Drive, Dropbox, Outlook, Asana, Trello, etc.

I bet you recognize many of those apps. I'm even willing to bet you use some of them in your day-to-day working life. Slack made that bet too. By being compatible with all of these apps, Slack makes itself indispensable. It allows businesses to use all of the software they need to run effectively in one place.

That's huge for attracting new clients because Slack has a "central hub" that makes using all of its software easier.

It's also huge for client retention.

Just think about how much work it would take to stop using Slack once you have it all set up and integrated with dozens of other apps. Add to that the cost of replacing Slack and training your people to use whatever you replace it with.

It all adds up, doesn't it? It adds up so much that you're likelier to stick with Slack. That's the power of embedded integration.

By making your service compatible with as many related services as possible, you give potential clients a big reason to sign up. And once they're signed up, that compatibility will make it very difficult for them to justify leaving.

HOW WILL YOU GROW YOUR SUBSCRIPTION SERVICE?

I want you to consider this question as we wrap up this chapter.

I've given you four powerful techniques I'm using right now. One of them is the technique I think is the most effective, especially for those who don't have bags of cash at their disposal. (Hint: It's the one that made up most of the chapter.)

Now, it's up to you to figure out which techniques could support your subscription business. Maybe you could use all of them. Perhaps only a couple could work for your model.

Whatever the case, you need to have *something* to add to your message and value proposition to ensure you keep growing your client numbers. I've given you four techniques, and I have 200-plus more in *Feed a Starving Crowd* if you want to go even deeper.

But for now, we're going to switch over to another important topic:

Once you have 'em, what will do to keep 'em coming back?

ACTION EXERCISE:

Which of the growth strategies will you implement for your business?

_____

_____

_____

_____

_____

CHAPTER NINE

HOW TO KEEP 'EM COMING BACK: MINIMIZING CHURN AND MAXIMIZING USAGE

I'm going to kick this chapter off with three words.

If you can achieve what these three words give you, your business can build a moat the size of the Atlantic Ocean.

What are those three words?

Net. Negative. Churn.

Churn is one of the biggest killers of subscription businesses. No matter how well you do at sales and marketing, your business will fail if you can't keep your subscribers.

Good businesses aim to lower their churn rates as much as possible. *Great* businesses shoot for net negative churn.

Take Shopify as an example.

This brilliant e-commerce platform consistently reports monthly retention rates of more than 100 percent. That means they're making more from their retained clients than they're losing from those who leave.

That's net negative churn. Revenue grows so consistently that your growth covers any losses you would have had due to churn.

SendGrid is another excellent example.

This communications platform is all about helping businesses speak directly to their customers via email. Its API service seamlessly integrates into many software packages and allows users to make their email campaigns as effective as possible.

What are its net dollar retention rates?

112 percent in 2015...

111 percent in 2016...

And a staggering *117 percent* in 2017.

Net negative churn.

That's what you're shooting for when building a subscription business. It's not enough to try to lower your churn rate as much as possible. You need to make sure your dollar retention rates are so high that the churn you do have doesn't impact your bottom line.

Net negative churn means your business is making more money than it loses.

WHY NET NEGATIVE CHURN AND EXPANSION REVENUE IS SO APPEALING

Let's kick things off with some questions.

What is net negative churn?

Net negative churn occurs when the amount of new revenue your business generates from existing customers is higher than the revenue you lose from cancellations and downgrades.

In other words, you're making more than you're losing.

What about this "expansion revenue" thing I touched on earlier?

Expansion revenue is money you make selling more to your existing customers—for example when someone signs up for a more expensive membership tier. It also includes money you make from cross-selling related products.

Combining net negative churn with expansion revenue makes your business much more appealing.

REDUCING CHURN—THE FOUR KEY TIPS FOR SUBSCRIPTION BUSINESSES

Now, we come to the meat of the chapter.... How do you create net negative churn?

We'll dig a little deeper with essential tips and examples to help you create net negative churn.

Tip #1 – Understand the Net Negative Churn Formula

Before you can even think about what you need to do to create net negative churn, you need to know how to calculate it.

After all, you can't actionably improve what you don't measure. That would be like trying to figure out how long a journey would take when you don't know where you're starting from. So, we have a simple formula for net negative revenue that uses your monthly recurring revenue (MRR) figures:

(Churned MRR – Expansion MRR / Starting MRR) x 100 = Net Dollar Retention Rate

You're looking for your Expansion MRR to be higher than your churned MRR. As long as that's the case, you have net negative churn.

Here's an example.

We assume your subscription business has 1,000 customers, each paying $20 per month. That gives you a Starting MRR of $20,000.

During the month, twenty of your existing clients cancel their subscriptions.

That leaves you with a Churned MRR of $400.

However, thirty of your existing clients upgraded to a higher membership tier, meaning they're now paying $50 per month. This gives you an Expansion MRR of $1,500.

Plugging all of that into our formula gives us:

(400 − 1500 20,000) x 100 = -5.5% Revenue Churn

Your MRR is $21,100, and you have a net negative churn rate of 5.5 percent.

Run this formula every month and look for both higher Expansion MRR and a negative number to pop out at the end of the calculation.

Tip #2 – Use Upselling and Cross-Selling

"Would you like fries with that?"

It's such a common phrase that almost anybody who hears it knows exactly where it comes from—McDonald's.

This one phrase may be the most famous example of upselling in history. Everybody who buys a burger at McDonald's will get hit with this simple question. And a considerable portion of them will spend the extra dollar or two on fries.

That's the beauty of both upselling and cross-selling. You're offering your customer something related to what they're already buying. That means they're more likely to buy it.

Head to Amazon and you'll see more examples.

Check out a product on Amazon, and Amazon will immediately show you which products customers often buy with it. Head to the Amazon home page while you're logged in to your account, and you will see product suggestions based on previous purchases.

Amazon wants you to buy more stuff. And it will try to make that happen by showing you items its algorithms think you'll like.

Upselling and cross-selling are some of the oldest tricks in the business book. But they're also some of the most effective, which is why you've got to think about ways to use them in your subscription business.

Do you have an additional service your customers could benefit from? Let them know.

Is there a higher tier to your membership that offers more value to a user? Tell them about it.

Anything you have beyond your base pricing package is something you may be able to upsell or cross-sell to your existing clients. Tell them the benefits and make offers. Not everybody will accept. But you'll get far more people buying more from you by being active here than you would by waiting for people to buy more on their own.

Spotify gives us a fantastic example of this.

If you're using the platform's free tier, you're cut off from using certain features. But Spotify won't hide those features from you. Instead, it will allow you to discover them. And when you find a feature you can't access, you'll get a little message telling you that you've found a Premium feature.

All you need to do is upgrade to Spotify Premium, and you can unlock it.

So, the user tries to do something because that offers some extra value; Spotify tells them they can't and then upsells them on the Premium package.

It's simple. It's easy.

And you can bet it gets many people signing up to access premium features.

Tip #3 – Expand Your Resources

Expanding your resources means offering more of what you're already offering.

Take Dropbox as an example.

If you sign up for its Basic package, you get 2 GB of cloud storage. That's pretty awesome because it gives you space to store essential documents.

But maybe you end up needing more space. Perhaps you want to store your music collection—or you make videos and want to have backups in the cloud.

That's okay.

Dropbox can give you even more storage. Just sign up to Dropbox Plus, and you get 2,000 GB.

Need more?

The Professional tier gives you 3,000 GB. And if you're running a business, you can subscribe to a tier that offers 5,000 GB.

Nothing super-special is going on here. Dropbox is just offering you more of what you're already using. It knows you need it, so it's going to make it as easy to upgrade as possible. Just one click of a button, and you're on your way…for a little extra money!

Expanding your resources lets you make more money from existing customers without having to introduce tons of new products and services. If you have a service that naturally scales up based on usage (like Dropbox), then you're in a great position to use this tip.

One final thing before we move on to the next tip.

Did you notice that I wrote out 2,000 GB, 3,000 GB, and 5,000 GB when talking about Dropbox's tiers? I did that because of the numbers Dropbox shows on its upgrade page.

Now, 2,000 GB is the same as 2 TB, 3,000 GB is the same as 3 TB, and so on.

Why doesn't Dropbox say 2 TB instead of 2,000 GB? It's because 2,000 GB seems bigger, even though it's the same as 2 TB!

Very clever Dropbox! Little marketing strategies like this sell people when you're using the expanded resources strategy.

Tip #4 – Leverage Customer Marketing Data

SaaS startup Groove had a problem.

It brought in plenty of new users—but it had a churn rate of 4.5 percent. Which meant its growth was unsustainable. Simply put, Groove was losing too much money because it couldn't keep its existing clients.

So, what did it do?

It got funky with its user analytics!

...

...

Sorry, that was terrible.

HOW GROOVE REDUCED CHURN BY 71 PERCENT WITH A SIMPLE EMAIL

Groove started parsing through all the data it collected about its users to identify what it called "Red Flag" metrics. These were metrics that subscribers who abandoned the platform tended to show patterns in.

Examples included login frequency and session length.

The latter was critical. Groove discovered that users who abandoned the platform tended to spend thirty-five seconds on a session. Those who stuck around spent an average of more than three minutes per session.

This data hinted at issues that could lead to churn.

For example, low session times (especially early on) might hint that a customer didn't complete the setup process. So, Groove sent out emails to this segment of its customer base, offering to set up a short Skype chat to help.

The subscriber gets better customer service. Groove gets a chance to sell the subscriber on the quality of its platform. It's a win-win!

Groove made similar offers to customers it believed could get more out of Groove if they knew about every feature it had.

The result of this data-driven approach?

Groove reduced churn by 71 percent because its data helped it figure out why subscribers were leaving. And once it knew why, Groove could do something about it.

The message with this final tip is simple:

Don't ignore your data!

It can tell you a lot about why people aren't sticking around (or why they are) so you can focus on improving your platform to reduce churn.

IMPLEMENTING A MODERN LOYALTY PROGRAM

Customer loyalty.

In the quest for net negative churn, loyalty is the secret ingredient. Loyal customers stick with you for the long haul, spend more money with you, and recommend your business to friends, family, and colleagues.

Loyalty is what you want.

And knowing that, you might feel like a loyalty program is in order. We've all seen the typical loyalty schemes in operation. A department store gives you a little card that gets swiped whenever you purchase. Eventually, you build up enough points to get a discount or gift.

It's simple, easy, and works…but it's not the most effective approach for a subscription business. Instead, look into the more modern loyalty methods companies use today. And I have the perfect example…

Uber!

A DEEP DIVE INTO UBER'S BRILLIANT MODERN SPIN ON LOYALTY PROGRAMS

Uber took the traditional points system and implemented tiers with its Uber Rewards program.

Although it has since discontinued the program, here's how it worked.

You earned points whenever you got an Uber or ordered from Uber Eats. So far, sounds familiar.

The number of points varied depending on what you ordered. You would get one point per dollar spent for an Uber Eats order. But you earned three points per dollar if you used Uber Premium.

This was the first twist to the traditional points system.

Uber offered members of its loyalty program more points for using the services that cost a little more. This was just a gentle nudge toward the company's premium services.

Building on this, the program had four tiers:

1. Blue
2. Gold
3. Platinum
4. Diamond

Each tier had a set number of points to accumulate during any loyalty program period to qualify. What's more, each of these tiers offered different benefits.

In the Blue tier, you didn't get a whole lot. This entry-level tier allowed you to earn points and, if you were lucky, get occasional access to special offers. It was a landing spot for new program members, with the low rewards motivating them to move up.

Gold was where things got interesting. You needed 1,200 points to get into this tier, so you likely spent close to $1,000 with Uber during a program period. This tier received rewards from Uber—and its program partners. Gold members also received a 10 percent discount on an Uber Comfort trip.

Then came Platinum. You needed 4,000 points to access this tier, equivalent to a couple of thousand dollars more spent. At this point, Uber was raking in the money from the loyalty program member. The reward for this loyalty was the Price Confidence perk. Platinum members could choose a route they regularly took, such as a commute to work, and nail down a standard price for it. That price might fluctuate a little during peak times. But even if that happened, Platinum members got a 35 percent discount.

And last, there was Diamond—accessible with 7,500 points. Here, you got everything you'd get from Platinum, plus free rideshare upgrades and access to premium phone support.

What Uber did was essentially create a membership within its loyalty program. Uber was encouraging people to spend more with it to unlock better rewards. It was a brilliant modern spin on the basic loyalty program points system.

Your long-term customers are your most valuable customers. And with a good loyalty program, you get to reward them, keep them happy, and benefit from their continued business (and referrals) for years to come.

Uber Rewards gave us a basic blueprint to follow for creating a tiered rewards program.

Interestingly, just as this book was getting ready to go to print, Uber announced it is ending its loyalty program in favor of a subscription program.[1]

Now, I want to give you a few more tips to enhance your loyalty program further.

Tip #1 – Focus on Existing Customers as Much as (If Not More Than) New Customers

In 2014, Lenovo purchased the IBM X86 server division. This purchase also gave it access to the division's business partners, who would be tasked with continuing to sell these servers under the Lenovo brand.

There was just one problem.

Lenovo's new partners weren't clear on the new direction. And without an incentive, they might have moved on to other opportunities. Now, Lenovo could have let them go while investing time and money into forming new partnerships. But they didn't want to lose partners loyal to the X86 division in the past. So, they created the Lenovo Expert Achievers Program (LEAP).

LEAP contained educational modules that rewarded participants with points for completion. It also included a sales dashboard into which existing partners could enter sales to get more points. Of course, those points were exchangeable for rewards at a later date.

---

1 - https://techcrunch.com/2022/08/14/uber-to-sunset-free-loyalty-program-in-favor-of-subscription-membership/

The result of this program? Seven hundred firms signed up and collectively sold seven times the number of products they had the year before. Lenovo crushed its target revenue figure of $170 million by 40 percent.

So, what's the point of this story? Taking care of existing customers is good for business.

By using a loyalty program to make the transition from IBM to Lenovo as simple as possible, Lenovo ended up with happier partners who worked harder to sell their server products.

In your case, focusing on existing clients is crucial to maintaining a core customer base for your subscription business. If you're constantly chasing new clients and neglecting the ones you already have, you're creating a recipe for churn.

Tip #2 – Leverage Personalization

Designer Shoe Warehouse (DSW) has a simple and convenient online loyalty program. Its customers automatically earn points with every purchase, meaning they don't need to worry about fooling around with complex systems.

It's brilliant.

But that level of automation made it possible for some customers to forget they were simply part of a loyalty scheme!

So, DSW came up with a great idea. It launched an email campaign to remind people about the program. The masterstroke here is that each email a customer received contained personalized information. It told them how many points *they* needed for their following $10 certificate. It also told them about the rewards *they* were currently eligible for.

In short, DSW focused on the individual.

Keep this in mind when you're designing your loyalty program. Your subscription clients aren't going to feel too loyal if you're sending them the same generic messages you send to everybody else. A little personalization goes a long way in ensuring your clients don't feel like just another number.

Tip #3 – Curate Your Rewards

Sticking with this little theme of not being generic, we have The North Face's loyalty program.

Again, we see a company sticking to a tried-and-true points system. But the twist here comes in rewards curation. The company's loyal members don't end up with access to a bunch of rewards offered to everybody.

They get rewards that mean something to them.

For example, a member who enjoys hiking trips in cold weather will get offers for special boots and limited-edition collections—based on their interests. The North Face uses customer data to make its loyalty offerings more appealing.

The lesson: You're collecting data about every one of your subscribers—use it to figure out what each person likes. What are their habits? What do they value most about your service?

Answer those questions, and you can start tailoring your rewards to the individual's needs.

Tip #4 – Build Tiers into Your Programs

We've already seen how Uber uses a tiered loyalty system.

It's far from the only company that does so.

Beauty company Sephora has a very similar structure. In its case, tiers range from the free Insider tier to VIB, and the top tier, Rouge. Members move up by spending money on Sephora products. If they spend $1,000 or more, they get access to Rouge, which offers seasonal savings, free shipping on any order, and a points exchange program.

Tiers work for several reasons.

For your business, they give you a chance to set thresholds for your loyalty rewards. Sephora only gives its best rewards to people who spend $1,000 or more with the company. Uber reserves its killer loyalty packages for people who accumulate 7,500 points in a system that pays a maximum of 3 points per dollar spent.

We see companies guarantee themselves a certain income before they start paying it back!

Tip #5 – Build a Community Through Your Program

When people feel part of an exclusive community, they're more likely to stick around.

The Body Shop does a great job building community around their Love Your Body Club.

On the surface, this program acts much like any other loyalty program—the more members spend, the more points they get, etc.

The difference lies in the sense of community the program creates. Members get access to exclusive events where they can meet other members. They get invited to parties and earn gift vouchers on their birthdays. These little events let people create ties with other members of the loyalty program, leading to that sense of community that's difficult to break away from.

In this book, we've already discussed the power of community for a subscription business. This is another way to leverage it to keep your existing clients around.

KEEPING CUSTOMERS HAPPY—BEST PRACTICES FOR SUBSCRIPTION BUSINESSES

Great loyalty programs keep customers happy because they get rewarded for participating in your business. Using your marketing data to make relevant offers or to expand your resources keeps people comfortable by giving them more of what they want.

If they're happy, they'll stick with you.

It's that simple.

So, let's inject a little more happiness into your subscription business. With these best practices, you stand a better chance of putting smiles on customers' faces.

Practice #1 – Know How Your Customers Define Success

How do you define customer success in your subscription business?

Trick question! You don't.

Your customers define what success means to them. Your job is to ensure your product or service facilitates their desired success.

The challenge is you often won't know what success is to your customers. This can lead to you making assumptions about what customers want instead of being sure.

How do you solve the problem? You could try asking customers what they want.

It's such a simple solution. But it's one most don't even think to try. Your customers can tell you exactly how they define success. Use surveys, send questionnaires, and start talking to the people who represent what your subscription business needs to offer.

Practice #2 – Have a Dashboard to Help You Track Metrics (Such as Product Usage Stats)

You may have heard of Box—it's a cloud storage company. Kind of like Dropbox with a slightly different name.

A few years ago, Box had a problem. It had been using Salesforce to determine why customers were leaving its platform. This led to it creating what it called "churn events." Knowing what these events were enabled Box to develop campaigns designed to minimize the impact of these churn events.

So far, so good.

The problem was Box struggled to use Salesforce to measure the success of its countermeasures. To solve that problem, it implemented a dashboard solution from a company called Gainsight.

These dashboards gave Box visibility into product adoption, usage statistics, and metrics that told it whether its churn event countermeasures were working. One of the dashboards revealed top clients at risk of not renewing in the next ninety days—an excellent shortlist for the customer success team to focus on.

The lesson for you as a subscription business owner? Dashboards give you valuable data at a glance.

You can quickly see what's going well and what's not by implementing dashboards related to your customer success metrics. You'll be able to spot negative usage patterns that clue you into areas where your clients aren't happy.

And once you know about those patterns, you can do something about them!

Practice #3 – Develop Onboarding and Offboarding Processes

Signing up a subscriber isn't over after their first payment.

You must onboard everybody who comes into your business—including your customers. The exact processes you follow will vary based on your type of business and model. But on a general level, you want to tell the new client what they can expect from your service, where they have to go to get what they need, and whom they should contact if they need help.

Offboarding is a little different.

This isn't you saying adios to a client on their way out. It's you doing what you can to understand what made the client want to leave and, hopefully, figuring out what you can do to convince them to stay or ensure the same problem doesn't happen to another client.

Offboarding processes should include questionnaires about why they're leaving and anything else that helps you understand their departure. Ideally, if the customer value is high enough, you would attempt to get on a call, understand their concerns, and see if you can find a way to keep them.

Practice #4 – Quickly Get to the First "Aha!" Moment

One thing that's important to do is help get the subscriber to their first "Aha!" moment—as quickly as possible.

When somebody signs up, make sure you're contacting them regularly—emails, phone calls, whatever it takes. Keep up a high touch rate to ensure the new client is getting everything they need.

For example, Wishpond is an all-in-one marketing platform, and its "Aha!" moment is when a user designs a landing page or contest, hits publish, and realizes it has a live campaign it can share with its audience. Wishpond found this from looking at its analytics data and asking customers where they found value.

To get users to this "Aha!" faster, Wishpond removed steps so customers could click the publish button with less friction. It also created premade templates to make it easier and added live chat for answering user questions.

Alpha Software enables companies to build mobile apps that work offline. Its users' "Aha!" moment comes when they first see an app working robustly offline. It's such a unique and well-loved feature that Alpha Software secured a patent for the technology!

Cloud Campaign is a social media platform for marketing agencies. Its "Aha!" moment is when a marketing agency can see a white-labeled one-click report with its logo. This enables agencies to charge a higher retainer for social media services.

Find your subscriber's "Aha!" moment—and get them there as quickly as possible.

Practice #5 – High Touch for the First 90 Days

The last thing you want is for your new subscribers to feel like you've forgotten about them.

Now, there's a balance to strike here.

I know I'd get sick of a company messaging me every hour. Eventually, those messages would start falling on deaf ears. So, you want to maintain high touch regularly without being so overbearing that clients start tuning you out.

Practice #6 – Segment Your Customer Base

When job search site Monster.com decided it wanted to expand deeper into the small business sector in 2017, it faced some significant challenges. Perhaps the largest involved reducing churn as it moved into a market it was less familiar with.

Reducing churn started with creating a better onboarding process.

But the key to the company's success was figuring out it needed to segment its customer base.

Monster.com used a customer success platform named Totango to segment its small business customers into three distinct groups. By doing that, it could track the activity of each group to understand its purchasing activity on the Monster platform. The company collected a ton of customer health data, allowing it to see product usage stats to understand better how to appeal to its customers.

With that data, Monster then focused on making simple (and relevant) offers to each segment. For example, if a customer was running low on job listings, it would trigger the customer rep to contact the client and top up their listings. It also created an overall health score for each client to determine who was most at risk.

The result? Reduced churn—because customers were getting relevant offers.

Relevant offers tie into the personalization points we discussed earlier. When sending generic offers to clients, you're telling them you don't know anything about who they are or what they want. Using a customer success platform to segment your audience, you can start tracking crucial metrics that highlight behavioral patterns for each segment.

Building from that data, you can make offers based on what the data tells you, rather than assumptions about what your clients may want.

Practice #7 – Create a Feedback Loop

What are your clients telling you about your subscription product or service?

What do you mean you don't know? Let's get that sorted out!

Feedback is a critical component in keeping your customers happy. If your subscribers feel like you're not listening to their concerns, they will go find somebody who will listen.

Translation...they'll stop paying you and start paying somebody else.

That's why you've got to set up a feedback loop. Give clients the means to get in touch with you—contact forms, customer care numbers, social media, whatever other tools you can think of.

This is such an essential practice that at Archistar, we created a weekly "Voice of the Customer" meeting. At the meetings, our customer success team runs through all the reasons customers decided to leave in the preceding week. Representatives from all the different departments are present so the entire business knows what's going on.

Now, here's the critical part.... Make sure you keep talking to clients.

You can't create a feedback loop if it's just clients sending messages to your company. You need to let clients know you've received their messages and keep them updated on what you're doing to solve their problems.

And once you have a solution, ask them about it. Talk to them about what you've implemented, what works for them, and what else they want to see change.

Keep the feedback loop going; you'll collect all the information you need to iterate your product and keep customers happy.

HOW WILL YOU KEEP AND GROW YOUR CUSTOMER BASE?

The main takeaway is that you can only have net negative churn when you have happy customers. To create satisfied customers, you must focus just as intently on the people who've already signed up as you do on your next customers.

This gives you the client retention and new client intake you need to have net negative churn.

You think everything I've spoken about in this chapter sounds like lots of work?

I won't lie to you.... It is!

But I'd like to leave this chapter with a final point. Many of the best subscription services don't need to do many of the things I've spoken about here. Take Slack as an example. I've used Slack for several years, and I love it.

But I've never had a Slack account manager. I've never taken part in a Slack training session. I'm almost sure I didn't get a ninety-day check-in, and I'm not a part of any Slack loyalty programs.

So...why do I stick around?

Because the service is so simple, easy to use, and effective that I don't need any of that stuff!

This shows that having an easy-to-use product and a strong market fit means you may not need to be as active in customer success.

But it takes time (and many good ideas) to get to where Slack is. While building your business, the techniques, practices, and tips I've shared in this chapter will help nudge you ever closer to net negative churn.

ACTION EXERCISE:

What actions will you take to retain and grow your customers?

_____

_____

_____

_____

CHAPTER TEN

ARE YOU ON TRACK? HOW TO KNOW IF YOU HAVE PRODUCT/MARKET FIT

I've touched on the concept of product/market fit at several points in this book. A product that matches the market you're trying to serve is a crucial aspect of building that all-important moat around your subscription business.

But what is a good product/market fit? The answer is simple.

Having a good product/market fit means you've managed to create a subscription offering that people want. Your offer fits the market so well that your ideal customers sign up because they're getting all the value they could need from you.

Every robust subscription business has a strong product/market fit. And to prove it, I'm going to kick off this chapter by hitting you with some examples of when businesses discovered they had product/market fit.

NETFLIX'S EVOLUTION INTO A SUBSCRIPTION MODEL

"That will never work."

Over and over, Netflix co-founder Marc Randolph heard that message when he introduced the concept of mail-order DVD rentals. Even his wife had almost zero confidence in the idea.

And you know what? All of those dissenting voices were right!

The first few iterations of Netflix's model didn't work because they didn't provide product/market fit. While the seed of a good idea was there, it would take much experimentation to push Netflix toward what we know it as today.

Adding little benefits—no due dates and late fees—helped massively. At the time, Netflix was competing with big rental stores like Blockbuster. By removing some of the annoying parts of being a Blockbuster customer, Netflix started carving out a niche.

Then came the idea for a subscription.

Give Netflix a certain amount of money per month, and you could rent as many DVDs as you wanted. Now the company was getting closer to that perfect product/market fit. People liked the idea of paying a monthly subscription for unlimited movie access.

Marc has this to say about the implementation of Netflix's subscription model:

"If there was a moment when Netflix stopped being a start-up and became a real company, it was then."

Engagement shot up. Churn dropped like a stone. Netflix was a real business!

Soon after came the advent of viable consumer streaming. Before anybody else, Netflix jumped on that bandwagon, finding a way to deliver movies digitally to subscribers' homes without needing to mess around with delivering and returning physical DVDs.

Finally, the platform had the final piece of its product/market puzzle:

Convenience.

The result.... (You don't need me to tell you, do you?)

Just pop into your local Blockbuster store to see the result of Netflix achieving the perfect product/market fit. Oh, wait...you can't!

Netflix decimated the old video rental market and became the top dog in the new video streaming market.

LOOKER AND THE BIG MARKET SHIFT

American software company Looker launched with a unique proposition for the business intelligence sector.

It wasn't trying to provide simple analytics tools to major businesses—Looker was a more developer-oriented analytics platform. It allowed engineers to fiddle around with the back-end to get the data they wanted to see on the (more user-friendly) front-end.

That's not an easy sell in a market that values convenience.

And that's what Looker discovered initially. After twelve months of pre-launch selling, the platform had just ten customers when it finally went to market.

They didn't have product/market fit…yet.

But in Looker's case, the market evolved to make its product viable. After about five months, two things happened that helped Looker succeed.

First, a new generation of data professionals started entering companies. And they wanted more control over the data they accessed and used, which Looker's back-end tools gave them in spades.

The second shift happened because of another company: Amazon Web Services. AWS released a new form of cloud-based data warehousing called Redshift soon after Looker launched. For the first time, warehousing became an option for many smaller businesses that couldn't previously afford the physical hardware needed to create a data warehouse.

The data landscape started changing.

And suddenly, Looker had a product that offered a great product/market fit.

The lesson from this story is that a good idea may be ahead of its time. But sometimes, product/market fit can occur because you've gotten ahead of the game. Staying the course when you have a good idea may be all you need to do if you know market forces are at play to make your subscription business viable.

PATREON AND THE OVERWHELMING CUSTOMER RESPONSE

Earlier, I dug into Patreon's story in detail, so I'm not going to say much about it here. You know the basics.

Jack Conte co-founded Patreon.

He created a YouTube video, which was one of many on his channel. And in the description of that video, he encouraged viewers to support him via the new platform he helped create.

A bunch of viewers did. And a new business was born!

Patreon CTO, President, and co-founder Samuel Yam tells us exactly when he and Jack knew they had product/market fit:

"For Patreon, it was right after we launched with Jack's music video on YouTube and patrons and creators started writing in.

"I'd never seen that level of passion and immediate resonance, and our launch was particularly fraught with stress since weeks before all the creators that were asked to launch rejected us."

This is a bit of an odd one.

On the one hand, the massive response from creators told the duo they were onto something. On the other hand, the rejections from creators sent them mixed messages.

Still, the power of that initial response couldn't be denied. And today, many successful content creators have a Patreon account.

This little story tells you something significant about product/market fit.

You're not always going to know whether you have it or not when you launch your product or service. But you can be sure your customers will tell you one way or the other.

Listen to them, even if you encounter some early obstacles. If you have people telling you your idea's fantastic, you're on your way to product/market fit.

GITHUB'S USERS ASK TO PAY

GitHub had a simple plan when it launched its private beta.

Offer it for free, and people will come.

And people certainly did come. But they came with an off request, as the company's co-founder Tom Preston-Werner points out:

"To our surprise, users started writing to us asking, 'Can we pay for this?' They liked it so much they wanted to pay for it. That was the first sign this was going to work."

That sounds like a pretty solid product/market fit to me. If customers are asking to pay for what you're offering, you're onto a winner.

There's not much more I can say about this one other than that it reinforces the message I shared about Patreon:

Your audience will tell you when you have a product/market fit.

Patreon was told it had a good fit when its ideal customers flooded it with messages.

GitHub got an even more unmistakable message:

Let us pay for it so that this thing can be even better!

Now, you're probably wondering why I'm telling you these stories.

It's because product/market fit isn't always a tangible thing you can apply metrics to. Sometimes, you know you have product/market fit because the market's telling you you're onto something.

The simple fact is product/market fit is the key to a subscription business. If what you're offering doesn't fit the market's needs, you don't have a business.

You have a product or service that won't sell, no matter how clever it is.

SUPERHUMAN—HOW RAHUL FOUND PRODUCT/MARKET FIT FOR THE FASTEST EMAIL IN THE WORLD

Rahul Vohra knew a product that won't sell is a failure, so achieving a product/market fit was at the top of his agenda when preparing to launch Superhuman.

The Superhuman value proposition was a simple one:

Provide the fastest email experience in the world.

But like many entrepreneurs, Rahul found himself bogged down in a sea of information as he searched for the ever-elusive fit. The year was 2017, and Rahul spent a ton of his time researching, reading articles and posts by thought leaders on business subjects, and achieving product/market fit.

He struggled to find anything that told him what product/market fit was. But Rahul discovered one post on Netscape founder Marc Andreessen's blog that he connected with. Andreessen wrote:

"You can always feel when product/market fit is not happening. The customers aren't quite getting value out of the product, word of mouth isn't spreading, usage isn't growing that fast, press reviews are kind of 'blah,' the sales cycle takes too long, and lots of deals never close."

That was a feeling Rahul knew all too well.

He and his software engineers had been working on Superhuman since 2015. They'd poured their hearts and souls into the project and had yet to reap any fruits of their labour.

Superhuman hadn't even launched yet!

And the reason it hadn't launched was that Rahul felt product/market fit wasn't going to happen for the product, at least in its current state. Even though he faced massive pressure to launch from himself and his team, he couldn't let go of the feeling that the fit wasn't there yet.

So, he started thinking.

Rahul asked himself what he would need to know to determine if he had product/market fit before launch. After all, that's what none of the articles he was reading could tell him. They all talked about how to know if you have a fit post-launch. But by then, it's often too late to do anything about a poor fit. The die is cast, the first impression is made, and many potential customers have fallen by the wayside.

That's the situation Rahul wanted to avoid, so he devised a survey.

That survey was sent out to every pre-launch user of the Superhuman platform to help Rahul see just where the product was in terms of its fit with the market. The survey contained four simple questions:

1. How would you feel if you could no longer use Superhuman?
    a. Very disappointed
    b. Somewhat disappointed
    c. Not disappointed
2. What type of people do you think would most benefit from Superhuman?
3. What is the main benefit you receive from Superhuman?
4. How can we improve Superhuman for you?

When the results came in, Rahul saw a disheartening number....

Only 22 percent of current users would feel "Very disappointed" if they could no longer use Superhuman. Rahul's suspicions were correct—the product/market fit wasn't quite there yet. But thanks to his survey, he now had some ideas about what he could do to achieve the fit.

Rahul got to work.

And eventually, he distilled all of his ideas into a few simple steps that helped Superhuman achieve the level of product/market fit that has resulted in a valuation of $825 million today.

These are the steps:

Step #1 – Find Your Supporters and Create a Persona for Your High-Expectation Clients

During the early stages of your business, you'll attract many different types of clients. Frankly, not all those clients will be a good fit for your subscription business.

Those are the people you want to weed out so you can focus on the ones who are good fits.

Segmenting your existing client base into groups is the way to do that. Focus specifically on the people who aren't getting what they need from your product. Talk to them about why that is. Sometimes, it's because your product isn't a good fit for them. In others, you're going to find that your most disappointed users are the ones who have the highest expectations because they've identified your product or service as being ideal for what they need.

They're just not happy with your execution.

Those are the people you want to create buyer personas for. Let them tell you what they need for your product to live up to their expectations. More often than not, this group of people will steer you closer to achieving a good fit.

Step #2 – Figure Out Why People Love the Product

By going the same survey route as Rahul, you'll likely see that you have some clients who love what you're doing and some who are on the fence.

You want more of the fence-sitters to turn into product fanatics.

So, talk to the people who love your product first. Find out what they adore about it and focus on building that out more. Couple that with focusing on the issues that your high-expectation users have and you will end up with a two-pronged effect.

You improve what's great while fixing what isn't working.

Start by building a roadmap that prioritizes the things you need to put in place to improve your product/market fit. Publicize that roadmap. Tell your users what you're working on and the timeframes involved. This will ensure the fence-sitters and high-expectation users can see that you are working on improvements.

Then, make it all happen.

I know saying that sounds a little blasé. But there's no better way to put it. Once you see what needs work, the only thing you can do is buckle down and get it done.

Step #3 – Measure, Repeat, Succeed

There is no such thing as the perfect product or service.

How do I know?

Think back to the stories I shared at the beginning of this chapter. In several of them, changing market forces and sentiments were vital to achieving product/market fit.

The message is simple: What fits today may not work tomorrow.

Following your roadmap leaves you with a product that is a much better fit for the market than when you started. But don't rest on your laurels. Measure your product/market fit and repeat these steps at least once per year. Keep talking to your clients to figure out what they love, what isn't working, what you can improve, and what you can add to make them stay in love with the service.

In the previous chapter, I discussed establishing a feedback loop as an essential best practice for a subscription business.

Here is where that loop comes into its own.

MAKING SUBSCRIPTION BUSINESSES WORK ON SMALL BUDGETS

We've looked at many businesses in this book.

I've given you case studies of multi-billion-dollar companies that have combined subscription with a moat to generate billions more in profit. We've also looked at several examples of smaller start-ups that became significant players in their industries.

But I know you may have a little inertia going on right now.

Perhaps you think some of the examples I've shared so far don't reflect the reality of your business. You don't have millions of dollars to invest in your idea. Is building a subscription business even possible for you if you're not already successful or you're not in a position to attract funding?

Can you make a subscription business work on a small budget?

Yes, you can!

And to prove it, I'm going to wrap up this book by inviting you to sit around my little imaginary fire to listen to some more stories. Only now, we're not going to focus on big, branded businesses that made subscriptions work.

We're going to look at some of the little guys.

Some of the smaller businesses started on a shoestring and became successful from hard work and the power of the subscription model.

Let's kick things off with…

HOW THE FOOD BOSS ACADEMY STARTED SUBSCRIPTION ON A SHOESTRING BUDGET

Lauryn Bright's idea for a business came from her own experiences.

A student who was also working full-time, Lauryn let her focus on nutrition lapse as the stress she was under started weighing heavily on her. She began putting on weight.

Eventually, a trip to the doctor gave her the wake-up call she needed. Her diet and lack of exercise meant she had high blood pressure. She'd need to be on medication for life to treat the problem.

That moment is crystalized in Lauryn's memory.

The moment led to her starting a journey that eventually resulted in losing ninety-seven pounds. But in a business sense, it's the start of a journey that would ultimately lead to her figuring she could help other people struggling with the same issues she faced.

Lauryn's experiences led to her founding of The Food Boss Academy.

A subscription program, The Food Boss Academy is an educational resource that gives subscribers step-by-step instructions on how to eat healthily to avoid the health issues Lauryn faced.

The program offers monthly modules with videos. Lauryn holds weekly live training sessions and provides each subscriber bi-weekly access to her so they can ask questions. Monthly group coaching sessions, all of which are downloadable, are just another way Lauryn adds value to her clients.

Today, Lauryn isn't stressed out by working full-time for somebody else.

She doesn't need to be.

Her food coaching subscription business has been successful enough for her to turn it into a full-fledged career. She's helping hundreds of people with food issues while collecting recurring monthly revenue.

And she did it without having to spend thousands of dollars.

The Lesson:

How did Lauryn manage to build a successful subscription business on a budget?

By taking the same approach she took to changing her diet. This is also the same approach she takes when working with clients…

Start small.

Business success doesn't happen overnight. In creating a subscription business, you're likely building something you've never worked with before. There's a lot to learn and a ton of mindset work that goes into creating a subscription business, especially when you're on a budget.

Don't try to run before you can walk.

Start small with a proof of concept and an introductory offer. Determine if your offer has a product/market fit and focus on delighting your first few clients. Encourage feedback and use it to build at your own pace.

People with bigger budgets will get where they want to go faster. But that doesn't mean you're never going to get there. Don't pressure yourself to spend money you don't have when starting.

A LOW-COST ONLINE RETAILER BOLTS ON SUBSCRIPTION

Ruslan Kogan's story is a real rags-to-riches tale. It's the sort of story that every broke entrepreneur dreams of. Only in Ruslan's case, that dream is now his reality.

Ruslan's parents arrived in Australia in 1989 with $90 in their pockets and a dream of giving their son a better life. The young Ruslan grew up in a Housing Commission flat in the outer suburbs of Melbourne, where he quickly started developing an interest in technology.

This interest blossomed when he built his first computer at nine years old.

A year later, young Ruslan had started his first business. As a ten-year-old, he'd collect lost golf balls, give them a clean, and then package them up in egg cartons to sell to golfers over the weekend. This first taste of entrepreneurship encouraged him to start more small businesses in his teens, including a web design agency and a mobile phone repair business.

And he did it all on a shoestring.

Those businesses earned Ruslan a little money. So, too, did the IT positions he'd eventually hold with General Electric and Bosch. But at twenty-three, Ruslan wanted more. Drawing from his love of technology, Ruslan founded kogan.com to sell leading consumer brands at lower prices than you'd find in most stores.

Ruslan started the enterprise in his parents' garage when he was twenty-three.

Today, Ruslan is worth hundreds of millions.

Now, you're probably wondering why I'm focusing on this guy. It sounds like his business was built around single-sale products rather than a subscription. And it was. But in more recent years, kogan.com unveiled its Kogan First membership.

For $59 per year, subscribers get access to rewards, discounts, free shipping, and exclusive deals. Ruslan has taken a business with a strong moat of offering consumer electronics at bargain prices and added the all-important subscription element to make it even stronger.

The Lesson:

You don't have to start with a subscription model.

As powerful as the subscription model is, it's not the only one out there. And if you're operating with a tiny budget, it may not be the best model to start with. In some cases, beginning with a business that focuses on making single sales can help you to build the capital needed to add a subscription element.

That's the approach Ruslan took.

Subscription is the gold standard. It's the model that reinforces your moat. But it's not the only business model out there.

When you're starting, subscription may not be the most effective model for you. Remember that other models have ceilings regarding earning potential and their appeal to investors. Use them to generate the capital you need to launch a subscription service.

HOW PATRICK TURNED A NINE-MONTH "EXPERIMENT" INTO A $200M EXIT

Nine months.

That's how long Patrick Campbell gave himself to see if this "being an entrepreneur" thing could work for him. Having spent time at Google, he had some of the technical skills needed to build a subscription business.

His new business was called Price Intelligently.

Patrick's company would provide businesses with the information they could use to tweak their prices and maximize sales. It was a simple concept, but it was one Patrick believed had some legs.

After all, pricing is one of the most challenging aspects of running a business.

Get it wrong and you either tank your business due to low sales or grow without making a profit because your margins are terrible. Patrick's idea would help companies grow sustainably while maintaining pricing models that worked for customers.

Patrick got to work, spending eighteen hours per day building his software and trying to publicize it. He wrote content, shot videos, and did everything he could to create a buzz.

And it worked.

A tech journalist at *The Boston Globe* found one of his posts and ended up running with Patrick's story, giving him some crucial exposure as he worked on his business idea.

Price Intelligently was now known in the market.

And happily for Patrick, it achieved the all-important product/market fit. More and more clients needed the data his service could extract. And as time went on, the professional services arm kept growing.

Then came another idea.

What if Patrick could provide more than just pricing data? What if he could also provide critical financial metrics related to churn and MRR?

That idea led to the birth of ProfitWell and the transformation of Patrick's businesses into a subscription model. With ProfitWell, Patrick offers a freemium solution where users get access to basic financial metrics and can pay more into their subscription to gain access to deeper metrics.

Users can subscribe to ProfitWell without having to pay a dollar for it.

But if they want to upgrade to the Enterprise package, which provides customization and more tailored results, they need to pay a subscription.

It's a model that's working. Today, ProfitWell boasts an average customer lifetime value of $150,000. That's *per customer*!

And it all started because a young man took a chance on himself and dedicated time to doing all the small jobs entrepreneurs often avoid.

Patrick recently sold ProfitWell to Paddle for $200 million. A great result and well deserved.

The Lesson:

You don't necessarily need to spend tons of money on expensive marketing firms to get to where you need to go.

Patrick didn't.

He realized he could do a lot of what those firms do himself. That's why he set aside time each week to write blog posts and tell his story. He knew that doing this himself lent his emerging brand a sense of authenticity that people might connect with.

And it worked.

Granted, nobody can guarantee that a journalist from a major newspaper will pick up on your blog posts and articles. But that doesn't mean you shouldn't write them.

The content you create around your business idea may be what lands you your first few clients. And once you have those clients, you have revenue coming in. With that revenue, you can start to build and scale.

HOW MICHAEL TURNED AN EXCESS STOCK PROBLEM INTO A BILLION-DOLLAR BUSINESS

Michael Dubin was on a flight from New York to Los Angeles.

He'd just lost his job and had no real idea what he would do when he landed in LA. Sure, he had a vague idea about getting into the comedy business in some fashion. But he had no experience. He'd never even taken part in an open mic night. That idea seemed dead in the water before he'd even landed!

Michael arrived in LA and started taking on odd jobs. Directionless for a few months, Michael's life finally took a turn for the better when he received a message from a friend:

"Hey Michael, I have a warehouse filled with 250,000 razors from South Korea—any ideas on how to sell them?"

Michael's gears started turning.

He, along with so many men, had long been tired of the standard procedure of buying razors at stores. You had to go and grab somebody to get the big key to unlock the razor rack. Then, you'd spend $20 on a set of razors you knew weren't worth that money.

But what other options did you have? As it turned out, Michael had another option brewing in his head....

"What if I created a subscription service that sent blades to customers automatically every month, at a reasonable price?"

And with that, the idea for Dollar Shave Club was born.

But a good idea doesn't mean much if nobody knows about it. What's more, the subscription service he wanted to create would have to go up against the likes of Gillette and other established names in the razor industry. And they had years of history and multi-million-dollar budgets to their names.

Michael didn't have any of that.

But he did have a camera and that vague notion about getting involved in comedy.

He set up the camera and started filming little marketing skits for a company that wasn't yet launched. The most famous involved somebody off-camera asking Michael if the blades he wanted to sell were good.

His response:

*"No! They're f***ing great!"*

That video went viral. Dollar Shave Club launched off the back of the video, selling the stock of 250,000 razors Michael's friend had in just one day.

The company had its launch platform.

A few years later, in 2019, Michael Dubin sold his stake in the business for a cool $1 billion.

Not a bad result for somebody who started jobless and directionless.

The Lesson:

Do you have a talent for something bubbling away under the surface?

Michael Dubin did.

He had some comedic talent and a bit of experience creating marketing videos. And by combining those two talents, he made the viral video that allowed Dollar Shave Club to launch with near-instant success.

I'm not guaranteeing that your hidden talents will lead to the same level of success. But they may be able to help you to market your business.

If you have a writing talent, get typing. If you like making videos in your spare time, use that talent to create videos about your business. My point is it's often the little talents we keep locked away that can help us connect with our audiences.

That's what Michael did with his marketing videos. He told a story and made people laugh.

Combine that with a product people want and a service that is much more convenient than the existing model, and you have a winner.

SOME FINAL ADVICE FOR THE BOOTSTRAPPERS ON RAZOR-THIN BUDGETS

I'm not going to pretend it's easy to launch a subscription business when you don't have much money at your disposal.

It isn't.

But that doesn't mean it can't be done. All four of the examples I've just shared showcase people who launched successful subscription companies despite not having massive budgets or business connections.

You can do it too.

Building from the lessons I've shared, I'd like to offer some final nuggets of advice for anyone aiming to launch on a low budget.

The first is not to spend lots of money on a website.

Why? You don't need to!

Why spend thousands of dollars on professional website development when you can use a service like Wix, Webflow, or WordPress to build your site using a free template?

The money you save going down that route can be poured into the business.

And guess what?

Your clients aren't going to care that you have a cheap and templated website as long as your subscription offers them what they're looking for.

Secondly, if you're looking to build an online store, use Shopify.

Again, you get to build a website that you know will work without spending a ton of money upfront. And the subscription you pay to use Shopify makes the expenses of running your website much easier to handle.

Thirdly, doing it yourself is not a bad thing. We saw that with Patrick Campbell's blog posts. Do the work on the back-end of your website. Write your content. Film your videos. You can do these things without investing too heavily into marketing or ad agencies.

Plenty of off-the-shelf tools offer free or low-cost solutions to many of the challenges you'll deal with in the beginning.

Ultimately, my message isn't that you don't need money to scale a subscription business.

You do.

But a lack of money doesn't mean you can't get started. It's possible to build something while bootstrapping. And that something may just give you the foundation you need to make a profitable and attractive subscription business.

A FINAL NOTE

Are you ready to launch your subscription business?

After reading this book, I trust your answer is "yes!"

The subscription model isn't a catch-all that works for every single type of business. But I believe I've demonstrated that the many variations of this model make it versatile enough to work for far more industries and business ideas than you may have thought.

I've shown you why a subscription is the way to go.

I've discussed the various subscription models, potential pricing models, and what you need to do to dig a wide and deep moat that protects your subscription business from copycats.

All that's left now is to get started.

But I will not leave you to do it all on your own.

If you're interested in building on what you've learned from this book, I invite you to visit the free resources page I've created to dig deeper into all the stories and techniques I've shared here.

Please visit https://www.subscriptionplaybook.com/resources to access the free resources page.

I wish you all the best in your subscription journey and look forward to hearing about your success story.

ACTION EXERCISE:

Before you go, take this great opportunity to reflect and write down the first three things you plan to do to get started.

_____

_____

_____

_____

RESOURCES

Chapter One

Levinter, Adam. *The Subscription Boom.* Vancouver, Canada: Figure 1 Publishing, 2019. Kindle Edition.

https://finance.yahoo.com/news/warren-buffett-explains-moat-principle-164442359.html

https://www.businessinsider.com/buffett-on-moats-2016-4?r=US&IR=T

https://hbr.org/1996/01/what-i-learned-from-warren-buffett

https://www.andersonleneave.com/resources/pricing-a-business-ebit-or-ebitda

https://howtoplanandsellabusiness.com/how-to-value-a-business/ebitda-multiples-by-industry/

https://www.valentiam.com/newsandinsights/ebitda-multiples-by-industry

https://www.zuora.com/guides/three-reasons-wall-street-loves-recurring-revenue-models/

https://www.ftadviser.com/investments/2020/07/02/subscription-models-are-good-investments/

https://different.com.au/

Chapter Two

https://www.digitalcameraworld.com/uk/news/gopro-subscription-strategy-is-stellar-success-says-ceo

https://aws.amazon.com/blogs/media/prmbp-gopro-enhances-subscription-ecosystem-livestreaming-aws/

https://www.businesswire.com/news/home/20210622005421/en/Zuora-Supports-GoPro%E2%80%99s-Subscription-Program-hitting-Milestone-Moment-of-Surpassing-One-Million-Subscribers

https://www.zuora.com/our-customers/case-studies/gopro/

https://gopro.com/en/us/shop/subscribe-to-gopro-subscription/GoProPlusYearly.html

https://subta.com/gopro-surpasses-750000-subscribers-reaches-nearly-150-growth-in-one-year/

https://www.clearhaus.com/blog/7-subscription-models-why-you-should-sell-subscriptions/

https://www.theglobeandmail.com/news/toronto/an-invitation-to-eat-think-and-be-wary/article14169544/

https://www.theglobeandmail.com/news/toronto/in-pictures-looking-back-at-the-grano-speakers-series/article14169618/

https://www.yellowpages.ca/bio/Ontario/Toronto/Grano-Restaurant/716514.html

https://www.aims.ca/site/media/aims/Grano(1).pdf

https://chrisbaisch.medium.com/unpacking-the-subscription-economy-series-8-the-consumables-subscription-model-1d0ca182c343

https://www.vitable.com.au/

https://www.businessnewsaustralia.com/articles/vitamins-subscription-healthtech-vitable-nourished-by--5-5m-series-a-raise.html

https://www.the-outlet.com/posts/vitable-review-one-month-of-vitable

https://www.uscreen.tv/blog/subscription-business-models/

https://www.nma.art/faq/

https://artignition.com/new-masters-academy-review/

https://www.watchgang.com/FAQs

https://www.inc.com/annabel-acton/how-a-watch-subscription-startup-made-15-million-in-its-first-year.html

http://subscriptioncommerceinsider.com/

https://www.inc.com/anne-gherini/the-rise-of-rundle-a-new-trend-for-subscription-based-services.html

https://blog.fusebill.com/price-bundling-as-a-growth-tactic-for-your-subscription-business

https://www.lavellehair.com.au/freebies/hair-subscription-service/

https://www.ey.com/en_uk/financial-services-emeia/how-insurance-subscription-models-are-impacting-the-industry

https://www.babylonhealth.com/pricing

https://www.prospectmagazine.co.uk/science-and-technology/babylon-health-virtual-health-care-nhs-funding

https://www.techradar.com/uk/news/what-is-saas

https://nira.com/salesforce-history/

https://finance.yahoo.com/quote/CRM/

https://www.jdsupra.com/legalnews/minimum-volume-commitments-92565/

https://www.cbinsights.com/research/report/stripe-teardown/

Chapter Three

https://cpl.thalesgroup.com/blog/software-monetization/six-creative-companies-using-subscription-models-brilliant-ways

https://www.cnet.com/tech/computing/what-is-gopro-plus/

https://mixergy.com/interviews/live-with-manuel-suarez/

http://abovethecrowd.com/2011/05/24/all-revenue-is-not-created-equal-the-keys-to-the-10x-revenue-club/

https://www.salesforce.com/blog/paid-organic-marketing-strategy-blog/

https://www.profitwell.com/recur/all/calculate-and-reduce-cac

https://www.forbes.com/sites/forbescoachescouncil/2020/11/16/12-smart-ways-to-lower-the-cost-of-customer-acquisition/?sh=311f37ea4cf3

https://www.nfx.com/post/defensibility-most-value-for-founders/

https://www.newbreedrevenue.com/blog/7-examples-of-strong-brand-positioning-and-why-they-work

https://99designs.co.uk/blog/business/failed-startups/

http://abovethecrowd.com/2011/05/24/all-revenue-is-not-created-equal-the-keys-to-the-10x-revenue-club/

https://gatewaycfs.com/bff/avoiding-high-customer-concentration

https://core.ac.uk/download/pdf/145016788.pdf

https://www.linkedin.com/pulse/network-effects-case-study-huynh-ngoc-tram-nguyen-alice-/

https://venturebeat.com/2014/11/10/sharing-economy-series-how-udemy-ramped-up-without-paid-advertising/

https://expandedramblings.com/index.php/udemy-facts-statistics/

https://pdfcoffee.com/udemy-case-study-pdf-free.html

https://www.nfx.com/post/network-effects-bible

https://online.hbs.edu/blog/post/what-are-network-effects

https://neilpatel.com/blog/how-netflix-maintains-low-churn/

https://www.thewrap.com/netflix-customers-less-likely-to-ditch-service-than-other-streamers/#:~:text=As%20you%20probably%20noticed%2C%20Netflix's,7%25%20during%20that%20same%20time.

https://otter.ai/u/83bOF3aUGGyvg_VS9l_phwZ-l0Y

https://otter.ai/u/gvPo8HUE_50di9vbK0Mz6oKHx5A

https://www.nasdaq.com/articles/is-peloton-building-a-true-competitive-advantage-2020-06-14

https://researchci.com/the-network-effect-why-pelotons-community-is-its-secret-weapon-amidst-competition/

http://abovethecrowd.com/2011/05/24/all-revenue-is-not-created-equal-the-keys-to-the-10x-revenue-club/

https://www.smartcompany.com.au/business-advice/strategy/five-steps-to-get-a-sustainable-competitive-advantage/

http://www.capatcolumbia.com/Articles/FoFinance/Fof1.pdf

https://backlinko.com/peloton-users

https://www.freshbooks.com/hub/accounting/calculate-gross-margin

http://abovethecrowd.com/2011/05/24/all-revenue-is-not-created-equal-the-keys-to-the-10x-revenue-club/

https://company-announcements.afr.com/asx/wtc/31853fd4-052c-11ec-bb32-12633425e3c4.pdf

https://uk.sports.yahoo.com/news/robust-financials-driving-recent-rally-043335990.html

https://www.startupdaily.net/2020/08/wisetech-shares-go-ballistic-after-fy20-results/

https://www.nfx.com/post/defensibility-most-value-for-founders/

https://corporatefinanceinstitute.com/resources/knowledge/accounting/marginal-profit/

https://au.investing.com/analysis/eight-key-factors-to-look-for-in-successful-companies-200172447

https://technologyonecorp.com/resources/media-releases/technologyone-full-year-results-for-2020

https://www.strategyzer.com/blog/posts/2015/7/27/switching-costs-6-strategies-to-lock-customers-in-your-ecosystem

https://www.nasdaq.com/articles/stripe%3A-the-internets-most-undervalued-company-2020-09-01

https://www.cbinsights.com/research/report/stripe-teardown/

Chapter Four

https://www.cbinsights.com/research/report/subscription-business-model-industries/#Airlines

https://www.subscriptiondna.com/blog/subscription-pricing-strategy-optimizing-pricing-model-subscription-business/

https://www.is.com/community/case-studies/pickcrafter/

https://makeawebsitehub.com/websites-with-ads/

https://www.is.com/mobile-app-advertising/

https://ebizfacts.com/pewdiepie-profile/

https://www.smartinsights.com/digital-marketing-strategy/online-retail-sales-growth/

https://gleam.io/blog/catch/

https://www.intelligentreach.com/blog/the-growth-of-catch-marketplace-au/

https://blog.mirakl.com/catch-group-marketplace-strategy-drives-a-winning-acquisition

https://fourweekmba.com/amazon-business-model/

https://www.bigcommerce.co.uk/articles/ecommerce/types-of-business-models/

https://www.ecommerceceo.com/types-of-ecommerce-business-models/

https://spendmenot.com/blog/paypal-statistics/#:~:text=6.,in%20net%20revenue%20in%202020.&text=During%20the%20third%20quarter%20of,quarter%20of%20the%20previous%20year.

https://www.statista.com/statistics/277841/paypals-total-payment-volume/

https://www.purchasecommerce.com/blog/payment-processing-companies

https://mixergy.com/interviews/abbey-escrow-interview/

https://avc.com/2013/01/mba-mondays-revenue-models-transaction-processing/

https://www.businessofapps.com/data/paypal-statistics/

https://businessesgrow.com/2016/12/06/big-data-case-studies/

https://tomroth.com.au/databiz/

https://businessesgrow.com/2016/12/06/big-data-case-studies/

https://tomroth.com.au/databiz/

https://bigthink.com/the-present/is-spotify-spying-on-you/

https://www.ggrecon.com/guides/is-the-fortnite-crew-subscription-worth-it/#:~:text=Fortnite%20Crew%20is%20a%20monthly,and%20a%20Fortnite%20Crew%20Pack.

https://www.digitalmediastream.co.uk/blog/10-saas-companies-who-rocked-the-freemium-model

https://techcrunch.com/2012/11/04/should-your-startup-go-freemium/

https://bmtoolbox.net/patterns/freemium/

https://productled.com/blog/free-trial-vs-freemium/#:~:text=Freemium%20is%20a%20customer%20acquisition,a%20limited%20amount%20of%20time

https://www.profitwell.com/recur/all/freemium-tradeoffs

https://www.profitwell.com/recur/all/blog/freemium/

https://blog.hubspot.com/service/freemium

https://www.cnet.com/how-to/good-reasons-to-pay-for-spotify/

https://larrycheng.com/2015/04/15/the-least-useful-slide-in-the-pitch-deck-is/

https://www.saastr.com/you-need-50-million-users-for-freemium-to-actually-work/

https://blog.hubspot.com/service/freemium

https://www.subscriptiondna.com/blog/annual-vs-monthly-billing-whats-the-best-pricing-model/

https://www.priceintelligently.com/blog/bid/194370/boosting-mrr-annual-vs-monthly-subscriptions-in-your-saas-pricing-strategy

Chapter Five

https://www.procore.com/pricing

https://www.procore.com/jobsite/understanding-procores-pricing-model/

https://www.insightpartners.com/blog/how-usage-based-pricing-fueled-two-2020-ipos/

https://paddle.com/blog/net-dollar-retention/

https://baremetrics.com/blog/usage-based-pricing

https://openviewpartners.com/blog/usage-based-pricing-playbook/#.YR9m2o5KhPY

Chapter Six

https://www.nfx.com/post/the-nfx-of-trulia-building-a-3-5-billion-marketplace/

https://www.businessinsider.com/pete-flint-trulia-nfx-vc-firm-150-million-early-stage-startup-fund-2017-11?r=US&IR=T

https://smallbusiness.chron.com/definition-industry-standard-model-15638.html

https://www.nfx.com/post/14th-network-effect-expertise/

https://whichrealestateagent.com.au/real-estate-agents-sydney/

https://www.nfx.com/post/10-years-about-market-networks/

https://www.nfx.com/post/media-marketplaces/

https://www.fourthsource.com/ai/the-rise-of-the-digital-media-marketplace-23134

https://www.nirandfar.com/the-curse-of-the-network-effect/

https://blogs.cornell.edu/info2040/2020/11/13/network-effects-in-the-gaming-console-industry/

https://stickybranding.com/how-brand-names-become-verbs/

https://www.businessinsider.com/companies-with-names-that-have-become-verbs-2018-7?r=US&IR=T

https://www.nfx.com/post/truth-about-data-network-effects/

https://www.styleseat.com/join/

https://brianbalfour.com/essays/the-network-effect-marketplaces

https://medium.com/@kaichentan/upwork-5d8de2636415

https://www.quora.com/How-does-Upwork-ensure-that-businesses-and-clients-dont-bypass-them-thereby-avoiding-payment-of-any-commissions

https://www.quora.com/How-does-TaskRabbit-make-sure-that-people-dont-hire-task-rabbits-outside-of-the-website-after-having-worked-with-them-to-avoid-the-15-fee-If-not-how-much-is-the-loss-of-that

https://www.growthengineering.co.uk/top-12-examples-of-gamification-in-business/

https://uxdesign.cc/game-design-as-a-product-development-framework-4d6cafa2bfdf

https://www.forbes.com/sites/forbestechcouncil/2018/11/15/smart-strategies-for-leveraging-gamification-within-your-business/?sh=27511ba93038

https://www.headway.io/blog/gamification-is-more-than-achievements

https://uxplanet.org/gamification-in-2017-top-5-key-principles-cef948254dad

Chapter Seven

https://support.patreon.com/hc/en-gb/articles/204606315-What-is-Patreon-#:~:text=For%20creators%2C%20Patreon%20is%20a,a%20creator%20on%20Patreon%20HERE.

https://www.sage.com/en-gb/blog/land-and-expand-strategy-saas/

https://mentomics.com/land-and-expand-then-explode/

https://www.saassales.io/executing-a-saas-land-and-expand-strategy/

https://www.docusign.co.uk/products-and-pricing

https://www.fool.com/investing/2021/09/01/this-companys-land-and-expand-business-model-shoul/

https://www.boldbusiness.com/digital/docusign-company-becoming-global-standard/

https://www.docusign.co.uk/blog/the-european-saas-opportunity

https://www.cnbc.com/2015/05/12/disruptor-docusign-raises-233m-for-global-trust-network.html

https://www.prnewswire.com/news-releases/docusign-global-trust-network-accelerates-with-125-yoy-customer-growth-300242141.html

https://www.businesswire.com/news/home/20130723005513/en/DocuSign-Trust-Network%E2%84%A2-Delivers-Secure-Platform-for-Global-Business-Transactions

Chapter Eight

https://www.wordstream.com/blog/ws/2016/04/27/value-proposition-examples

https://www.natalieluneva.com/blog/how-11-saas-companies-use-community-marketing-to-grow/

https://neilpatel.com/blog/boost-saas-growth-and-retention/

https://www.linkedin.com/pulse/use-webinars-grow-your-business-jeanette-spencer/

https://info.mezzaninegrowth.com/blog/ do-formal-referral-programs-increase-sales-for-b2b-companies

https://www.slideshare.net/jackmortonWW/jac-knew-realities

https://growsurf.com/blog/9-compelling-referral-marketing-statistics-you-need-to-know

https://www.workato.com/the-connector/ saas-growth-strategy/

https://referralrock.com/blog/ starting-your-saas-referral-program/

https://support.gusto.com/article/106622339100000/ Refer-a-friend-to-Gusto

https://help.dropbox.com/accounts-billing/space-storage/ earn-space-referring-friends

https://help.evernote.com/hc/en-us/ articles/208314268-Redeem-Evernote-Points

https://ontraport.com/partners/

http://slack.com/intl/en-gb/apps

https://www.elastic.io/saas-embedded-integration/

https://cyclr.com/blog/embedded-integration-who-does-what

Chapter Nine

https://medium.com/hackernoon/smb-saas-and-the-curious-case-of-negative-churn-da52b5ec730e

https://www.yannickoswald.com/post/why-are-investors-obsessed-with-churn

https://www.zuora.com/guides/three-reasons-wall-street-loves-recurring-revenue-models/

https://www.smartkarrot.com/resources/blog/expansion-revenue-mrr/#:~:text=Expansion%20revenue%20is%20the%20revenue,more%20than%20the%20initial%20purchase.&text=Expansion%20revenue%20is%20when%20revenue,to%20get%20the%20best%20results

https://baremetrics.com/blog/negative-churn#:~:text=What%20is%20net%20negative%20churn,lose%20from%20cancellations%20and%20downgrades

https://www.profitwell.com/recur/all/negative-churn

https://www.higherlogic.com/blog/what-is-net-negative-churn/

https://blog.bismart.com/en/the-most-successful-cases-of-cross-selling-and-up-selling

https://www.appcues.com/blog/upselling-prompts-saas

https://www.dropbox.com/space-upgrade?oqa=rnro&reason=upgrade

https://cxl.com/blog/reduce-churn/

https://www.pointhacks.com.au/uber-rewards/

https://thechampagnemile.com.au/uber-rewards-australia/

https://peertopeermarketing.co/b2b-loyalty-program/

https://www.shopify.com/blog/loyalty-program

https://sleeknote.com/blog/customer-loyalty-programs#1

https://www.helpscout.com/blog/saas-customer-success/

https://www.smartkarrot.com/resources/blog/top-10-customer-success-best-practices-for-saas/

https://www.custify.com/7-customer-success-best-practices-you-can-put-into-action

https://www.gainsight.com/customer/box/

https://www.totango.com/customers/monster

Chapter Ten

https://www.lennysnewsletter.com/p/what-it-feels-like-when-youve-found

https://blog.initialized.com/2021/06/the-metrics-you-need-to-raise-a-series-a/

https://burklandassociates.com/2020/01/31/sixteen-metrics-to-master-for-series-b/

https://www.calqulate.io/blog/growth-rate-valuation-series-b

https://blog.publiccomps.com/top-5-saas-metrics/

https://www.investopedia.com/articles/personal-finance/102015/series-b-c-funding-what-it-all-means-and-how-it-works.asp#series-b-funding

https://www.unionbank.com/commercial/insights/emerging-businesses/rarified-territory-series-c-raise-what-startups-need-to-know

https://corporatefinanceinstitute.com/resources/knowledge/valuation/startup-valuation-metrics-internet/

https://www.forbes.com/sites/alexkonrad/2021/08/04/superhuman-raises-75-million-for-its-waitlist-only-email-productivity-app/#:~:text=The%20round%2C%20which%20included%20Tiger,with%20knowledge%20of%20the%20transaction.

https://review.firstround.com/how-superhuman-built-an-engine-to-find-product-market-fit

https://www.tribehub.com/podcast/lauryn-bryght-food-boss-academy#

https://www.laurynbryght.com/food-boss-academy

https://www.kogan.com/au/ruslan-kogan/

https://www.smh.com.au/national/the-real-story-behind-315-million-ruslan-kogan-20140113-30pb9.html

https://www.kogan.com/au/kogan-first/

https://www.saastock.com/blog/from-price-intelligently-to-profitwell-how-a-saas-company-evolves/

https://www.profitwell.com/pricing

https://www.churn.fm/episode/how-profitwell-increased-their-customer-lifetime-value-from-6k-to-150k

https://sterlingwoods.com/blog/dollar-shave-club-story/

https://www.cnbc.com/2019/02/06/dollar-shave-club-ceo-michael-dubin-work-life-balance.html

FREE BOOK RESOURCES WEB PAGE

Some of the content couldn't fit on these pages, so I have collated it all into a free book resources page.

Visit https://www.subscriptionplaybook.com/resources to access:

1. The subscription model selector tool: Answer a few easy questions and receive a personalized recommendation about which subscription model is best suited to your business.
2. "Moat" Scorecard: A diagnostic tool where you can see how your business ranks in terms of the key factors to keep away competitors.
3. Pricing model recommendation tool: Find out which pricing model is the best fit for your business.
4. Screenshots of best practice subscription businesses.

To get all of this content and much more, go to https://www.subscriptionplaybook.com/resources

ABOUT THE AUTHOR

"One of the most influential online marketers around the globe."
— *The Huffington Post*

"An online marketing guru." — *Fast Company*

Robert Coorey, MBA, is a best-selling author, keynote speaker, and successful marketer. He is the co-founder of ArchiStar.ai, one of the world's fastest-growing property technology companies and the twentieth fastest-growing company in Australia as of December 2021, having raised more than $30 million in venture capital. In 2021, Robert was ranked #28 by *Business News Australia* in its list of Australia's Top 100 Young Entrepreneurs.

Robert has run marketing campaigns in more than 100 different industries. When running his marketing agency, he almost broke the world record for most people in a webinar. Robert was also the co-founder of World High Five Day, which was supported by former Australian Prime Minister Tony Abbott and other celebrities. He resides in Sydney, Australia with his wife and three children.

BE SURE TO READ FEED A STARVING CROWD

Double Your Business Revenue...

Without Advertising!

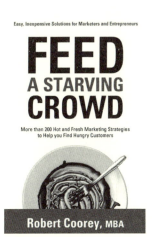

Do you lose sleep over wasting money on ads and promotions that fall flat? Do you wish you could crush it on social media, email, and your website? Want to know how to find and feed more customers than you can handle? If so, this book is for you!

Robert Coorey, MBA, has done the research and hard work. From deconstructing killer marketing campaigns to mastering the neuroscience and psychology of consumer activity, he shares brilliant, inexpensive strategies anyone can profit from.

You will learn how to:

- Get all the targeted traffic you can handle for pennies
- Launch like the big boys on a small business budget

- Master psychological tactics to create buyer frenzy
- Market like crazy on social media even though they say it's impossible
- Double customers' initial spending
- Sell out multi-million-dollar events without spending a dime on advertising
- Find starving crowds in your juiciest markets in minutes
- Profit from checkout procedures, landing pages, product choices

"This powerful, practical book is loaded with great ideas to help you sell more, faster and easier in any market."

— **Brian Tracy,** Author of *Unlimited Sales Success*

"An amazing collection of marketing hacks and shortcuts. The only issue with this book is that after reading each page, you feel the itch to put it down and rush to your laptop to start executing on the many wonderful ideas you learn."

— **Vishen Lakhiani,** Founder & CEO, Mindvalley

"Any one of the tested and proven strategies in this book will make you money. Taken as a whole, they are a roadmap to the peak of your business potential."

— **Patrick Snow,** International Best-Selling Author of *Creating Your Own Destiny* and *The Affluent Entrepreneur*